Texas State Notary Recordkeeping Book

TXNotaryForm.com

DEDICATION

This book designed to cover GOVERNMENT CODE, TITLE 4. EXECUTIVE BRANCH, SUBTITLE A. EXECUTIVE OFFICERS, CHAPTER 406. NOTARY PUBLIC; COMMISSIONER OF DEEDS. Sec. 406.014. NOTARY RECORDS. Including changes effective from January 01, 2025

ACKNOWLEDGMENTS

This book is designed to cover TEXAS GOVERNMENT CODE, TITLE 4. EXECUTIVE BRANCH, SUBTITLE A. EXECUTIVE OFFICERS, CHAPTER 406. NOTARY PUBLIC; COMMISSIONER OF DEEDS. Sec. 406.014. NOTARY RECORDS. Including changes effective from January 01, 2025

By TXNotaryForm.com

TEXAS STATE NOTARY RECORDKEEPING BOOK

Notary Public Commissioned Name

Notary ID	Records from Date	End Date

TXNotaryForm.com

HOW TO FILL OUT THE BOOK.

- Notarization Date – *Fill in the date when the signer appeared in front of you, either in person or remotely via video call.*
- Signer's, Grantor's, or Maker's Name – *Full legal name of Signer (Grantor or Maker).*
- Signer's, Grantor's, or Maker's mailing Address – *Signer's mailing address.*
    - Known – *Check if the Signer is personally known to the notary.*
    - Introduced– *Check if the Signer was introduced to the notary.*
        - ID Card/ ID+KBA- *Check if the Signer is unknown and not introduced. The Notary verifies an identification card issued by a governmental agency or a passport issued by the United States, or the Signer was identified using identity proofing and credential analysis.*
    - Exp.Date/Session ID – *Expiration date of document or session ID from identity proofing and credential analysis vendor.*
    - Meeting Type
        - Remote Online – *Check if it was Remote Online Notarization(RON).*
        - In-Person Meeting – *Check if it was an in-personal notarization.*
    - Document Type
        - Digital File – *Check if the notarized Document was digital or electronic files.*
        - Paper Document – *Check if notarized Document was tangible Document, paper document.*
- Brief description of the Document. If land is conveyed or charged, the name of the original grantee and the county where the land is located – *Please write the title and a brief description of the notarized Document; if the land was mentioned in the document, including the original grantee and the county where the land is located. Other notes.*
- Introducer's, Witness's Name and Mailing address, identification method (Known/Introduced/ID card/ID+KBA [Exp.Date/Session ID]) – *Please underline if witnessed or if the signer was introduced. In the event that the Signer was introduced, please include the name and mailing address of the introducer, as well as how they were identified. If notarization had a witness, please include the witness's name and mailing address, as well as how they were identified.(Known/Introduced/ID Card/ID+KBA).*
- Notarization County – *The notary must be physically present in Texas during the notarization process and specify the county where the notarization took place.*
- Document Date – *What is the date on the document?*
- Notarization Fee – *If the notary charged for notarization, what was the total amount the signer was charged for the service?*

Notarization Date	Signer's, Grantor's, or Maker's Name		
10/25/2024	Joe Doe		
○ Known ○ Introduced ⊗ ID Card/ID+KBA	Signer's, Grantor's, or Maker's mailing Address 567 North Main st. City, STATE, 12345		
Exp.Date/Session ID 02-15-32	Brief description of the Document. If land is conveyed or charged, the name of the original grantee and the county where the land is located Acknowledgment		
Meeting Type ○ Remote Online ⊗ In-Person Meeting	Introducer's, Witness's Name and Mailing address, identification method (Known/Introduced/ID card/ID+KBA [Exp.Date/Session ID])		
Document Type ○ Digital File ⊗ Paper Document	Notarization County Travis	Document Date 10/25/2024	Notarization Fee $35.00

Notarization Date	Signer's, Grantor's, or Maker's Name		
10/25/2024	Joe Doe		
⊗ Known ○ Introduced ○ ID Card/ID+KBA	Signer's, Grantor's, or Maker's mailing Address 567 North Main st. City, STATE, 12345		
Exp.Date/Session ID	Brief description of the Document. If land is conveyed or charged, the name of the original grantee and the county where the land is located Acknowledgment		
Meeting Type ⊗ Remote Online ○ In-Person Meeting	Introducer's, Witness's Name and Mailing address, identification method (Known/Introduced/ID card/ID+KBA [Exp.Date/Session ID])		
Document Type ⊗ Digital File ○ Paper Document	Notarization County Travis	Document Date 10/25/2024	Notarization Fee $35.00

Notarization Date	Signer's, Grantor's, or Maker's Name		
11/25/2024	James Doe		
○ Known ⊗ Introduced ○ ID Card/ID+KBA	Signer's, Grantor's, or Maker's mailing Address 89 EastMain st. Big City, STATE, 12345		
Exp.Date/Session ID	Brief description of the Document. If land is conveyed or charged, the name of the original grantee and the county where the land is located Acknowledgment		
Meeting Type ⊗ Remote Online ○ In-Person Meeting	Introducer's, Witness's Name and Mailing address, identification method (Known/Introduced/ID card/ID+KBA [Exp.Date/Session ID]) Joe Doe, known ,567 North Main st. City, STATE, 12345.		
Document Type ⊗ Digital File ○ Paper Document	Notarization County Travis	Document Date 10/25/2024	Notarization Fee $35.00

Notarization Date	Signer's, Grantor's, or Maker's Name		
○ Known ○ Introduced ○ ID Card/ID+KBA	Signer's, Grantor's, or Maker's mailing Address		
Exp.Date/Session ID	Brief description of the Document. If land is conveyed or charged, the name of the original grantee and the county where the land is located		
Meeting Type ○ Remote Online ○ In-Person Meeting	Introducer's, Witness's Name and Mailing address, identification method (Known/Introduced/ID card/ID+KBA [Exp.Date/Session ID])		
Document Type ○ Digital File ○ Paper Document	Notarization County	Document Date	Notarization Fee

Notarization Date

Signer's, Grantor's, or Maker's Name

O Known
O Introduced
O ID Card/ID+KBA

Exp.Date/Session ID

Signer's, Grantor's, or Maker's mailing Address

Brief description of the Document. If land is conveyed or charged, the name of the original grantee and the county where the land is located

Meeting Type
O Remote Online
O In-Person Meeting

Introducer's, Witness's Name and Mailing address, identification method (Known/Introduced/ID card/ID+KBA [Exp.Date/Session ID])

Document Type
O Digital File
O Paper Document

Notarization County	**Document Date**	**Notarization Fee**

Notarization Date

Signer's, Grantor's, or Maker's Name

O Known
O Introduced
O ID Card/ID+KBA

Exp.Date/Session ID

Signer's, Grantor's, or Maker's mailing Address

Brief description of the Document. If land is conveyed or charged, the name of the original grantee and the county where the land is located

Meeting Type
O Remote Online
O In-Person Meeting

Introducer's, Witness's Name and Mailing address, identification method (Known/Introduced/ID card/ID+KBA [Exp.Date/Session ID])

Document Type
O Digital File
O Paper Document

Notarization County	**Document Date**	**Notarization Fee**

Notarization Date

Signer's, Grantor's, or Maker's Name

O Known
O Introduced
O ID Card/ID+KBA

Exp.Date/Session ID

Signer's, Grantor's, or Maker's mailing Address

Brief description of the Document. If land is conveyed or charged, the name of the original grantee and the county where the land is located

Meeting Type
O Remote Online
O In-Person Meeting

Introducer's, Witness's Name and Mailing address, identification method (Known/Introduced/ID card/ID+KBA [Exp.Date/Session ID])

Document Type
O Digital File
O Paper Document

Notarization County	**Document Date**	**Notarization Fee**

Notarization Date

Signer's, Grantor's, or Maker's Name

O Known
O Introduced
O ID Card/ID+KBA

Exp.Date/Session ID

Signer's, Grantor's, or Maker's mailing Address

Brief description of the Document. If land is conveyed or charged, the name of the original grantee and the county where the land is located

Meeting Type
O Remote Online
O In-Person Meeting

Introducer's, Witness's Name and Mailing address, identification method (Known/Introduced/ID card/ID+KBA [Exp.Date/Session ID])

Document Type
O Digital File
O Paper Document

Notarization County	**Document Date**	**Notarization Fee**

Notarization Date	Signer's, Grantor's, or Maker's Name		
O Known O Introduced O ID Card/ID+KBA	**Signer's, Grantor's, or Maker's mailing Address**		
Exp.Date/Session ID	Brief description of the Document. If land is conveyed or charged, the name of the original grantee and the county where the land is located		
Meeting Type O Remote Online O In-Person Meeting	Introducer's, Witness's Name and Mailing address, identification method (Known/Introduced/ID card/ID+KBA [Exp.Date/Session ID])		
Document Type O Digital File O Paper Document	**Notarization County**	**Document Date**	**Notarization Fee**

Notarization Date	Signer's, Grantor's, or Maker's Name		
O Known O Introduced O ID Card/ID+KBA	**Signer's, Grantor's, or Maker's mailing Address**		
Exp.Date/Session ID	Brief description of the Document. If land is conveyed or charged, the name of the original grantee and the county where the land is located		
Meeting Type O Remote Online O In-Person Meeting	Introducer's, Witness's Name and Mailing address, identification method (Known/Introduced/ID card/ID+KBA [Exp.Date/Session ID])		
Document Type O Digital File O Paper Document	**Notarization County**	**Document Date**	**Notarization Fee**

Notarization Date	Signer's, Grantor's, or Maker's Name		
O Known O Introduced O ID Card/ID+KBA	**Signer's, Grantor's, or Maker's mailing Address**		
Exp.Date/Session ID	Brief description of the Document. If land is conveyed or charged, the name of the original grantee and the county where the land is located		
Meeting Type O Remote Online O In-Person Meeting	Introducer's, Witness's Name and Mailing address, identification method (Known/Introduced/ID card/ID+KBA [Exp.Date/Session ID])		
Document Type O Digital File O Paper Document	**Notarization County**	**Document Date**	**Notarization Fee**

Notarization Date	Signer's, Grantor's, or Maker's Name		
O Known O Introduced O ID Card/ID+KBA	**Signer's, Grantor's, or Maker's mailing Address**		
Exp.Date/Session ID	Brief description of the Document. If land is conveyed or charged, the name of the original grantee and the county where the land is located		
Meeting Type O Remote Online O In-Person Meeting	Introducer's, Witness's Name and Mailing address, identification method (Known/Introduced/ID card/ID+KBA [Exp.Date/Session ID])		
Document Type O Digital File O Paper Document	**Notarization County**	**Document Date**	**Notarization Fee**

Notarization Date	Signer's, Grantor's, or Maker's Name		
O Known O Introduced O ID Card/ID+KBA	Signer's, Grantor's, or Maker's mailing Address		
Exp.Date/Session ID	Brief description of the Document. If land is conveyed or charged, the name of the original grantee and the county where the land is located		
Meeting Type O Remote Online O In-Person Meeting	Introducer's, Witness's Name and Mailing address, identification method (Known/Introduced/ID card/ID+KBA [Exp.Date/Session ID])		
Document Type O Digital File O Paper Document	Notarization County	Document Date	Notarization Fee

Notarization Date	Signer's, Grantor's, or Maker's Name		
O Known O Introduced O ID Card/ID+KBA	Signer's, Grantor's, or Maker's mailing Address		
Exp.Date/Session ID	Brief description of the Document. If land is conveyed or charged, the name of the original grantee and the county where the land is located		
Meeting Type O Remote Online O In-Person Meeting	Introducer's, Witness's Name and Mailing address, identification method (Known/Introduced/ID card/ID+KBA [Exp.Date/Session ID])		
Document Type O Digital File O Paper Document	Notarization County	Document Date	Notarization Fee

Notarization Date	Signer's, Grantor's, or Maker's Name		
O Known O Introduced O ID Card/ID+KBA	Signer's, Grantor's, or Maker's mailing Address		
Exp.Date/Session ID	Brief description of the Document. If land is conveyed or charged, the name of the original grantee and the county where the land is located		
Meeting Type O Remote Online O In-Person Meeting	Introducer's, Witness's Name and Mailing address, identification method (Known/Introduced/ID card/ID+KBA [Exp.Date/Session ID])		
Document Type O Digital File O Paper Document	Notarization County	Document Date	Notarization Fee

Notarization Date	Signer's, Grantor's, or Maker's Name		
O Known O Introduced O ID Card/ID+KBA	Signer's, Grantor's, or Maker's mailing Address		
Exp.Date/Session ID	Brief description of the Document. If land is conveyed or charged, the name of the original grantee and the county where the land is located		
Meeting Type O Remote Online O In-Person Meeting	Introducer's, Witness's Name and Mailing address, identification method (Known/Introduced/ID card/ID+KBA [Exp.Date/Session ID])		
Document Type O Digital File O Paper Document	Notarization County	Document Date	Notarization Fee

Notarization Date	Signer's, Grantor's, or Maker's Name		
O Known O Introduced O ID Card/ID+KBA	**Signer's, Grantor's, or Maker's mailing Address**		
	Brief description of the Document. If land is conveyed or charged, the name of the original grantee and the county where the land is located		
Exp.Date/Session ID			
Meeting Type O Remote Online O In-Person Meeting	Introducer's, Witness's Name and Mailing address, identification method (Known/Introduced/ID card/ID+KBA [Exp.Date/Session ID])		
Document Type O Digital File O Paper Document	**Notarization County**	**Document Date**	**Notarization Fee**

Notarization Date	Signer's, Grantor's, or Maker's Name		
O Known O Introduced O ID Card/ID+KBA	**Signer's, Grantor's, or Maker's mailing Address**		
	Brief description of the Document. If land is conveyed or charged, the name of the original grantee and the county where the land is located		
Exp.Date/Session ID			
Meeting Type O Remote Online O In-Person Meeting	Introducer's, Witness's Name and Mailing address, identification method (Known/Introduced/ID card/ID+KBA [Exp.Date/Session ID])		
Document Type O Digital File O Paper Document	**Notarization County**	**Document Date**	**Notarization Fee**

Notarization Date	Signer's, Grantor's, or Maker's Name		
O Known O Introduced O ID Card/ID+KBA	**Signer's, Grantor's, or Maker's mailing Address**		
	Brief description of the Document. If land is conveyed or charged, the name of the original grantee and the county where the land is located		
Exp.Date/Session ID			
Meeting Type O Remote Online O In-Person Meeting	Introducer's, Witness's Name and Mailing address, identification method (Known/Introduced/ID card/ID+KBA [Exp.Date/Session ID])		
Document Type O Digital File O Paper Document	**Notarization County**	**Document Date**	**Notarization Fee**

Notarization Date	Signer's, Grantor's, or Maker's Name		
O Known O Introduced O ID Card/ID+KBA	**Signer's, Grantor's, or Maker's mailing Address**		
	Brief description of the Document. If land is conveyed or charged, the name of the original grantee and the county where the land is located		
Exp.Date/Session ID			
Meeting Type O Remote Online O In-Person Meeting	Introducer's, Witness's Name and Mailing address, identification method (Known/Introduced/ID card/ID+KBA [Exp.Date/Session ID])		
Document Type O Digital File O Paper Document	**Notarization County**	**Document Date**	**Notarization Fee**

Notarization Date	Signer's, Grantor's, or Maker's Name		
○ Known ○ Introduced ○ ID Card/ID+KBA	Signer's, Grantor's, or Maker's mailing Address		
Exp.Date/Session ID	Brief description of the Document. If land is conveyed or charged, the name of the original grantee and the county where the land is located		
Meeting Type ○ Remote Online ○ In-Person Meeting	Introducer's, Witness's Name and Mailing address, identification method (Known/Introduced/ID card/ID+KBA [Exp.Date/Session ID])		
Document Type ○ Digital File ○ Paper Document	Notarization County	Document Date	Notarization Fee

Notarization Date	Signer's, Grantor's, or Maker's Name		
○ Known ○ Introduced ○ ID Card/ID+KBA	Signer's, Grantor's, or Maker's mailing Address		
Exp.Date/Session ID	Brief description of the Document. If land is conveyed or charged, the name of the original grantee and the county where the land is located		
Meeting Type ○ Remote Online ○ In-Person Meeting	Introducer's, Witness's Name and Mailing address, identification method (Known/Introduced/ID card/ID+KBA [Exp.Date/Session ID])		
Document Type ○ Digital File ○ Paper Document	Notarization County	Document Date	Notarization Fee

Notarization Date	Signer's, Grantor's, or Maker's Name		
○ Known ○ Introduced ○ ID Card/ID+KBA	Signer's, Grantor's, or Maker's mailing Address		
Exp.Date/Session ID	Brief description of the Document. If land is conveyed or charged, the name of the original grantee and the county where the land is located		
Meeting Type ○ Remote Online ○ In-Person Meeting	Introducer's, Witness's Name and Mailing address, identification method (Known/Introduced/ID card/ID+KBA [Exp.Date/Session ID])		
Document Type ○ Digital File ○ Paper Document	Notarization County	Document Date	Notarization Fee

Notarization Date	Signer's, Grantor's, or Maker's Name		
○ Known ○ Introduced ○ ID Card/ID+KBA	Signer's, Grantor's, or Maker's mailing Address		
Exp.Date/Session ID	Brief description of the Document. If land is conveyed or charged, the name of the original grantee and the county where the land is located		
Meeting Type ○ Remote Online ○ In-Person Meeting	Introducer's, Witness's Name and Mailing address, identification method (Known/Introduced/ID card/ID+KBA [Exp.Date/Session ID])		
Document Type ○ Digital File ○ Paper Document	Notarization County	Document Date	Notarization Fee

Notarization Date	Signer's, Grantor's, or Maker's Name		
○ Known ○ Introduced ○ ID Card/ID+KBA	Signer's, Grantor's, or Maker's mailing Address		
Exp.Date/Session ID	Brief description of the Document. If land is conveyed or charged, the name of the original grantee and the county where the land is located		
Meeting Type ○ Remote Online ○ In-Person Meeting	Introducer's, Witness's Name and Mailing address, identification method (Known/Introduced/ID card/ID+KBA [Exp.Date/Session ID])		
Document Type ○ Digital File ○ Paper Document	**Notarization County**	**Document Date**	**Notarization Fee**

Notarization Date	Signer's, Grantor's, or Maker's Name		
○ Known ○ Introduced ○ ID Card/ID+KBA	Signer's, Grantor's, or Maker's mailing Address		
Exp.Date/Session ID	Brief description of the Document. If land is conveyed or charged, the name of the original grantee and the county where the land is located		
Meeting Type ○ Remote Online ○ In-Person Meeting	Introducer's, Witness's Name and Mailing address, identification method (Known/Introduced/ID card/ID+KBA [Exp.Date/Session ID])		
Document Type ○ Digital File ○ Paper Document	**Notarization County**	**Document Date**	**Notarization Fee**

Notarization Date	Signer's, Grantor's, or Maker's Name		
○ Known ○ Introduced ○ ID Card/ID+KBA	Signer's, Grantor's, or Maker's mailing Address		
Exp.Date/Session ID	Brief description of the Document. If land is conveyed or charged, the name of the original grantee and the county where the land is located		
Meeting Type ○ Remote Online ○ In-Person Meeting	Introducer's, Witness's Name and Mailing address, identification method (Known/Introduced/ID card/ID+KBA [Exp.Date/Session ID])		
Document Type ○ Digital File ○ Paper Document	**Notarization County**	**Document Date**	**Notarization Fee**

Notarization Date	Signer's, Grantor's, or Maker's Name		
○ Known ○ Introduced ○ ID Card/ID+KBA	Signer's, Grantor's, or Maker's mailing Address		
Exp.Date/Session ID	Brief description of the Document. If land is conveyed or charged, the name of the original grantee and the county where the land is located		
Meeting Type ○ Remote Online ○ In-Person Meeting	Introducer's, Witness's Name and Mailing address, identification method (Known/Introduced/ID card/ID+KBA [Exp.Date/Session ID])		
Document Type ○ Digital File ○ Paper Document	**Notarization County**	**Document Date**	**Notarization Fee**

Notarization Date	Signer's, Grantor's, or Maker's Name		
○ Known ○ Introduced ○ ID Card/ID+KBA	Signer's, Grantor's, or Maker's mailing Address		
Exp.Date/Session ID	Brief description of the Document. If land is conveyed or charged, the name of the original grantee and the county where the land is located		
Meeting Type ○ Remote Online ○ In-Person Meeting	Introducer's, Witness's Name and Mailing address, identification method (Known/Introduced/ID card/ID+KBA [Exp.Date/Session ID])		
Document Type ○ Digital File ○ Paper Document	Notarization County	Document Date	Notarization Fee

Notarization Date	Signer's, Grantor's, or Maker's Name		
○ Known ○ Introduced ○ ID Card/ID+KBA	Signer's, Grantor's, or Maker's mailing Address		
Exp.Date/Session ID	Brief description of the Document. If land is conveyed or charged, the name of the original grantee and the county where the land is located		
Meeting Type ○ Remote Online ○ In-Person Meeting	Introducer's, Witness's Name and Mailing address, identification method (Known/Introduced/ID card/ID+KBA [Exp.Date/Session ID])		
Document Type ○ Digital File ○ Paper Document	Notarization County	Document Date	Notarization Fee

Notarization Date	Signer's, Grantor's, or Maker's Name		
○ Known ○ Introduced ○ ID Card/ID+KBA	Signer's, Grantor's, or Maker's mailing Address		
Exp.Date/Session ID	Brief description of the Document. If land is conveyed or charged, the name of the original grantee and the county where the land is located		
Meeting Type ○ Remote Online ○ In-Person Meeting	Introducer's, Witness's Name and Mailing address, identification method (Known/Introduced/ID card/ID+KBA [Exp.Date/Session ID])		
Document Type ○ Digital File ○ Paper Document	Notarization County	Document Date	Notarization Fee

Notarization Date	Signer's, Grantor's, or Maker's Name		
○ Known ○ Introduced ○ ID Card/ID+KBA	Signer's, Grantor's, or Maker's mailing Address		
Exp.Date/Session ID	Brief description of the Document. If land is conveyed or charged, the name of the original grantee and the county where the land is located		
Meeting Type ○ Remote Online ○ In-Person Meeting	Introducer's, Witness's Name and Mailing address, identification method (Known/Introduced/ID card/ID+KBA [Exp.Date/Session ID])		
Document Type ○ Digital File ○ Paper Document	Notarization County	Document Date	Notarization Fee

Notarization Date	**Signer's, Grantor's, or Maker's Name**		
○ Known ○ Introduced ○ ID Card/ID+KBA	**Signer's, Grantor's, or Maker's mailing Address**		
Exp.Date/Session ID	Brief description of the Document. If land is conveyed or charged, the name of the original grantee and the county where the land is located		
Meeting Type ○ Remote Online ○ In-Person Meeting	Introducer's, Witness's Name and Mailing address, identification method (Known/Introduced/ID card/ID+KBA [Exp.Date/Session ID])		
Document Type ○ Digital File ○ Paper Document	**Notarization County**	**Document Date**	**Notarization Fee**

Notarization Date	Signer's, Grantor's, or Maker's Name		
○ Known ○ Introduced ○ ID Card/ID+KBA	**Signer's, Grantor's, or Maker's mailing Address**		
Exp.Date/Session ID	Brief description of the Document. If land is conveyed or charged, the name of the original grantee and the county where the land is located		
Meeting Type ○ Remote Online ○ In-Person Meeting	Introducer's, Witness's Name and Mailing address, identification method (Known/Introduced/ID card/ID+KBA [Exp.Date/Session ID])		
Document Type ○ Digital File ○ Paper Document	**Notarization County**	**Document Date**	**Notarization Fee**

Notarization Date	Signer's, Grantor's, or Maker's Name		
○ Known ○ Introduced ○ ID Card/ID+KBA	**Signer's, Grantor's, or Maker's mailing Address**		
Exp.Date/Session ID	Brief description of the Document. If land is conveyed or charged, the name of the original grantee and the county where the land is located		
Meeting Type ○ Remote Online ○ In-Person Meeting	Introducer's, Witness's Name and Mailing address, identification method (Known/Introduced/ID card/ID+KBA [Exp.Date/Session ID])		
Document Type ○ Digital File ○ Paper Document	**Notarization County**	**Document Date**	**Notarization Fee**

Notarization Date	Signer's, Grantor's, or Maker's Name		
○ Known ○ Introduced ○ ID Card/ID+KBA	**Signer's, Grantor's, or Maker's mailing Address**		
Exp.Date/Session ID	Brief description of the Document. If land is conveyed or charged, the name of the original grantee and the county where the land is located		
Meeting Type ○ Remote Online ○ In-Person Meeting	Introducer's, Witness's Name and Mailing address, identification method (Known/Introduced/ID card/ID+KBA [Exp.Date/Session ID])		
Document Type ○ Digital File ○ Paper Document	**Notarization County**	**Document Date**	**Notarization Fee**

Notarization Date	Signer's, Grantor's, or Maker's Name		
O Known O Introduced O ID Card/ID+KBA	**Signer's, Grantor's, or Maker's mailing Address**		
	Brief description of the Document. If land is conveyed or charged, the name of the original grantee and the county where the land is located		
Exp.Date/Session ID			
Meeting Type O Remote Online O In-Person Meeting	Introducer's, Witness's Name and Mailing address, identification method (Known/Introduced/ID card/ID+KBA [Exp.Date/Session ID])		
Document Type O Digital File O Paper Document	**Notarization County**	**Document Date**	**Notarization Fee**

Notarization Date	Signer's, Grantor's, or Maker's Name		
O Known O Introduced O ID Card/ID+KBA	**Signer's, Grantor's, or Maker's mailing Address**		
	Brief description of the Document. If land is conveyed or charged, the name of the original grantee and the county where the land is located		
Exp.Date/Session ID			
Meeting Type O Remote Online O In-Person Meeting	Introducer's, Witness's Name and Mailing address, identification method (Known/Introduced/ID card/ID+KBA [Exp.Date/Session ID])		
Document Type O Digital File O Paper Document	**Notarization County**	**Document Date**	**Notarization Fee**

Notarization Date	Signer's, Grantor's, or Maker's Name		
O Known O Introduced O ID Card/ID+KBA	**Signer's, Grantor's, or Maker's mailing Address**		
	Brief description of the Document. If land is conveyed or charged, the name of the original grantee and the county where the land is located		
Exp.Date/Session ID			
Meeting Type O Remote Online O In-Person Meeting	Introducer's, Witness's Name and Mailing address, identification method (Known/Introduced/ID card/ID+KBA [Exp.Date/Session ID])		
Document Type O Digital File O Paper Document	**Notarization County**	**Document Date**	**Notarization Fee**

Notarization Date	Signer's, Grantor's, or Maker's Name		
O Known O Introduced O ID Card/ID+KBA	**Signer's, Grantor's, or Maker's mailing Address**		
	Brief description of the Document. If land is conveyed or charged, the name of the original grantee and the county where the land is located		
Exp.Date/Session ID			
Meeting Type O Remote Online O In-Person Meeting	Introducer's, Witness's Name and Mailing address, identification method (Known/Introduced/ID card/ID+KBA [Exp.Date/Session ID])		
Document Type O Digital File O Paper Document	**Notarization County**	**Document Date**	**Notarization Fee**

Notarization Date	**Signer's, Grantor's, or Maker's Name**		
○ Known ○ Introduced ○ ID Card/ID+KBA	**Signer's, Grantor's, or Maker's mailing Address**		
Exp.Date/Session ID	Brief description of the Document. If land is conveyed or charged, the name of the original grantee and the county where the land is located		
Meeting Type ○ Remote Online ○ In-Person Meeting	Introducer's, Witness's Name and Mailing address, identification method (Known/Introduced/ID card/ID+KBA [Exp.Date/Session ID])		
Document Type ○ Digital File ○ Paper Document	**Notarization County**	**Document Date**	**Notarization Fee**

Notarization Date	Signer's, Grantor's, or Maker's Name		
○ Known ○ Introduced ○ ID Card/ID+KBA	**Signer's, Grantor's, or Maker's mailing Address**		
Exp.Date/Session ID	Brief description of the Document. If land is conveyed or charged, the name of the original grantee and the county where the land is located		
Meeting Type ○ Remote Online ○ In-Person Meeting	Introducer's, Witness's Name and Mailing address, identification method (Known/Introduced/ID card/ID+KBA [Exp.Date/Session ID])		
Document Type ○ Digital File ○ Paper Document	**Notarization County**	**Document Date**	**Notarization Fee**

Notarization Date	Signer's, Grantor's, or Maker's Name		
○ Known ○ Introduced ○ ID Card/ID+KBA	**Signer's, Grantor's, or Maker's mailing Address**		
Exp.Date/Session ID	Brief description of the Document. If land is conveyed or charged, the name of the original grantee and the county where the land is located		
Meeting Type ○ Remote Online ○ In-Person Meeting	Introducer's, Witness's Name and Mailing address, identification method (Known/Introduced/ID card/ID+KBA [Exp.Date/Session ID])		
Document Type ○ Digital File ○ Paper Document	**Notarization County**	**Document Date**	**Notarization Fee**

Notarization Date	Signer's, Grantor's, or Maker's Name		
○ Known ○ Introduced ○ ID Card/ID+KBA	**Signer's, Grantor's, or Maker's mailing Address**		
Exp.Date/Session ID	Brief description of the Document. If land is conveyed or charged, the name of the original grantee and the county where the land is located		
Meeting Type ○ Remote Online ○ In-Person Meeting	Introducer's, Witness's Name and Mailing address, identification method (Known/Introduced/ID card/ID+KBA [Exp.Date/Session ID])		
Document Type ○ Digital File ○ Paper Document	**Notarization County**	**Document Date**	**Notarization Fee**

Notarization Date	Signer's, Grantor's, or Maker's Name		
O Known O Introduced O ID Card/ID+KBA	Signer's, Grantor's, or Maker's mailing Address		
Exp.Date/Session ID	Brief description of the Document. If land is conveyed or charged, the name of the original grantee and the county where the land is located		
Meeting Type O Remote Online O In-Person Meeting	Introducer's, Witness's Name and Mailing address, identification method (Known/Introduced/ID card/ID+KBA [Exp.Date/Session ID])		
Document Type O Digital File O Paper Document	Notarization County	Document Date	Notarization Fee

Notarization Date	Signer's, Grantor's, or Maker's Name		
O Known O Introduced O ID Card/ID+KBA	Signer's, Grantor's, or Maker's mailing Address		
Exp.Date/Session ID	Brief description of the Document. If land is conveyed or charged, the name of the original grantee and the county where the land is located		
Meeting Type O Remote Online O In-Person Meeting	Introducer's, Witness's Name and Mailing address, identification method (Known/Introduced/ID card/ID+KBA [Exp.Date/Session ID])		
Document Type O Digital File O Paper Document	Notarization County	Document Date	Notarization Fee

Notarization Date	Signer's, Grantor's, or Maker's Name		
O Known O Introduced O ID Card/ID+KBA	Signer's, Grantor's, or Maker's mailing Address		
Exp.Date/Session ID	Brief description of the Document. If land is conveyed or charged, the name of the original grantee and the county where the land is located		
Meeting Type O Remote Online O In-Person Meeting	Introducer's, Witness's Name and Mailing address, identification method (Known/Introduced/ID card/ID+KBA [Exp.Date/Session ID])		
Document Type O Digital File O Paper Document	Notarization County	Document Date	Notarization Fee

Notarization Date	Signer's, Grantor's, or Maker's Name		
O Known O Introduced O ID Card/ID+KBA	Signer's, Grantor's, or Maker's mailing Address		
Exp.Date/Session ID	Brief description of the Document. If land is conveyed or charged, the name of the original grantee and the county where the land is located		
Meeting Type O Remote Online O In-Person Meeting	Introducer's, Witness's Name and Mailing address, identification method (Known/Introduced/ID card/ID+KBA [Exp.Date/Session ID])		
Document Type O Digital File O Paper Document	Notarization County	Document Date	Notarization Fee

Notarization Date	Signer's, Grantor's, or Maker's Name		
○ Known ○ Introduced ○ ID Card/ID+KBA	Signer's, Grantor's, or Maker's mailing Address		
Exp.Date/Session ID	Brief description of the Document. If land is conveyed or charged, the name of the original grantee and the county where the land is located		
Meeting Type ○ Remote Online ○ In-Person Meeting	Introducer's, Witness's Name and Mailing address, identification method (Known/Introduced/ID card/ID+KBA [Exp.Date/Session ID])		
Document Type ○ Digital File ○ Paper Document	Notarization County	Document Date	Notarization Fee

Notarization Date	Signer's, Grantor's, or Maker's Name		
○ Known ○ Introduced ○ ID Card/ID+KBA	Signer's, Grantor's, or Maker's mailing Address		
Exp.Date/Session ID	Brief description of the Document. If land is conveyed or charged, the name of the original grantee and the county where the land is located		
Meeting Type ○ Remote Online ○ In-Person Meeting	Introducer's, Witness's Name and Mailing address, identification method (Known/Introduced/ID card/ID+KBA [Exp.Date/Session ID])		
Document Type ○ Digital File ○ Paper Document	Notarization County	Document Date	Notarization Fee

Notarization Date	Signer's, Grantor's, or Maker's Name		
○ Known ○ Introduced ○ ID Card/ID+KBA	Signer's, Grantor's, or Maker's mailing Address		
Exp.Date/Session ID	Brief description of the Document. If land is conveyed or charged, the name of the original grantee and the county where the land is located		
Meeting Type ○ Remote Online ○ In-Person Meeting	Introducer's, Witness's Name and Mailing address, identification method (Known/Introduced/ID card/ID+KBA [Exp.Date/Session ID])		
Document Type ○ Digital File ○ Paper Document	Notarization County	Document Date	Notarization Fee

Notarization Date	Signer's, Grantor's, or Maker's Name		
○ Known ○ Introduced ○ ID Card/ID+KBA	Signer's, Grantor's, or Maker's mailing Address		
Exp.Date/Session ID	Brief description of the Document. If land is conveyed or charged, the name of the original grantee and the county where the land is located		
Meeting Type ○ Remote Online ○ In-Person Meeting	Introducer's, Witness's Name and Mailing address, identification method (Known/Introduced/ID card/ID+KBA [Exp.Date/Session ID])		
Document Type ○ Digital File ○ Paper Document	Notarization County	Document Date	Notarization Fee

Notarization Date | **Signer's, Grantor's, or Maker's Name**

○ Known
○ Introduced
○ ID Card/ID+KBA

Signer's, Grantor's, or Maker's mailing Address

Brief description of the Document. If land is conveyed or charged, the name of the original grantee and the county where the land is located

Exp.Date/Session ID

Meeting Type
○ Remote Online
○ In-Person Meeting

Introducer's, Witness's Name and Mailing address, identification method (Known/Introduced/ID card/ID+KBA [Exp.Date/Session ID])

Document Type
○ Digital File
○ Paper Document

Notarization County	**Document Date**	**Notarization Fee**

Notarization Date | Signer's, Grantor's, or Maker's Name

○ Known
○ Introduced
○ ID Card/ID+KBA

Signer's, Grantor's, or Maker's mailing Address

Brief description of the Document. If land is conveyed or charged, the name of the original grantee and the county where the land is located

Exp.Date/Session ID

Meeting Type
○ Remote Online
○ In-Person Meeting

Introducer's, Witness's Name and Mailing address, identification method (Known/Introduced/ID card/ID+KBA [Exp.Date/Session ID])

Document Type
○ Digital File
○ Paper Document

Notarization County	**Document Date**	**Notarization Fee**

Notarization Date | Signer's, Grantor's, or Maker's Name

○ Known
○ Introduced
○ ID Card/ID+KBA

Signer's, Grantor's, or Maker's mailing Address

Brief description of the Document. If land is conveyed or charged, the name of the original grantee and the county where the land is located

Exp.Date/Session ID

Meeting Type
○ Remote Online
○ In-Person Meeting

Introducer's, Witness's Name and Mailing address, identification method (Known/Introduced/ID card/ID+KBA [Exp.Date/Session ID])

Document Type
○ Digital File
○ Paper Document

Notarization County	**Document Date**	**Notarization Fee**

Notarization Date | Signer's, Grantor's, or Maker's Name

○ Known
○ Introduced
○ ID Card/ID+KBA

Signer's, Grantor's, or Maker's mailing Address

Brief description of the Document. If land is conveyed or charged, the name of the original grantee and the county where the land is located

Exp.Date/Session ID

Meeting Type
○ Remote Online
○ In-Person Meeting

Introducer's, Witness's Name and Mailing address, identification method (Known/Introduced/ID card/ID+KBA [Exp.Date/Session ID])

Document Type
○ Digital File
○ Paper Document

Notarization County	**Document Date**	**Notarization Fee**

Notarization Date	Signer's, Grantor's, or Maker's Name		
O Known O Introduced O ID Card/ID+KBA	Signer's, Grantor's, or Maker's mailing Address		
Exp.Date/Session ID	Brief description of the Document. If land is conveyed or charged, the name of the original grantee and the county where the land is located		
Meeting Type O Remote Online O In-Person Meeting	Introducer's, Witness's Name and Mailing address, identification method (Known/Introduced/ID card/ID+KBA [Exp.Date/Session ID])		
Document Type O Digital File O Paper Document	Notarization County	Document Date	Notarization Fee

Notarization Date	Signer's, Grantor's, or Maker's Name		
O Known O Introduced O ID Card/ID+KBA	Signer's, Grantor's, or Maker's mailing Address		
Exp.Date/Session ID	Brief description of the Document. If land is conveyed or charged, the name of the original grantee and the county where the land is located		
Meeting Type O Remote Online O In-Person Meeting	Introducer's, Witness's Name and Mailing address, identification method (Known/Introduced/ID card/ID+KBA [Exp.Date/Session ID])		
Document Type O Digital File O Paper Document	Notarization County	Document Date	Notarization Fee

Notarization Date	Signer's, Grantor's, or Maker's Name		
O Known O Introduced O ID Card/ID+KBA	Signer's, Grantor's, or Maker's mailing Address		
Exp.Date/Session ID	Brief description of the Document. If land is conveyed or charged, the name of the original grantee and the county where the land is located		
Meeting Type O Remote Online O In-Person Meeting	Introducer's, Witness's Name and Mailing address, identification method (Known/Introduced/ID card/ID+KBA [Exp.Date/Session ID])		
Document Type O Digital File O Paper Document	Notarization County	Document Date	Notarization Fee

Notarization Date	Signer's, Grantor's, or Maker's Name		
O Known O Introduced O ID Card/ID+KBA	Signer's, Grantor's, or Maker's mailing Address		
Exp.Date/Session ID	Brief description of the Document. If land is conveyed or charged, the name of the original grantee and the county where the land is located		
Meeting Type O Remote Online O In-Person Meeting	Introducer's, Witness's Name and Mailing address, identification method (Known/Introduced/ID card/ID+KBA [Exp.Date/Session ID])		
Document Type O Digital File O Paper Document	Notarization County	Document Date	Notarization Fee

Notarization Date	Signer's, Grantor's, or Maker's Name		
O Known O Introduced O ID Card/ID+KBA	Signer's, Grantor's, or Maker's mailing Address		
Exp.Date/Session ID	Brief description of the Document. If land is conveyed or charged, the name of the original grantee and the county where the land is located		
Meeting Type O Remote Online O In-Person Meeting	Introducer's, Witness's Name and Mailing address, identification method (Known/Introduced/ID card/ID+KBA [Exp.Date/Session ID])		
Document Type O Digital File O Paper Document	Notarization County	Document Date	Notarization Fee

Notarization Date	Signer's, Grantor's, or Maker's Name		
O Known O Introduced O ID Card/ID+KBA	Signer's, Grantor's, or Maker's mailing Address		
Exp.Date/Session ID	Brief description of the Document. If land is conveyed or charged, the name of the original grantee and the county where the land is located		
Meeting Type O Remote Online O In-Person Meeting	Introducer's, Witness's Name and Mailing address, identification method (Known/Introduced/ID card/ID+KBA [Exp.Date/Session ID])		
Document Type O Digital File O Paper Document	Notarization County	Document Date	Notarization Fee

Notarization Date	Signer's, Grantor's, or Maker's Name		
O Known O Introduced O ID Card/ID+KBA	Signer's, Grantor's, or Maker's mailing Address		
Exp.Date/Session ID	Brief description of the Document. If land is conveyed or charged, the name of the original grantee and the county where the land is located		
Meeting Type O Remote Online O In-Person Meeting	Introducer's, Witness's Name and Mailing address, identification method (Known/Introduced/ID card/ID+KBA [Exp.Date/Session ID])		
Document Type O Digital File O Paper Document	Notarization County	Document Date	Notarization Fee

Notarization Date	Signer's, Grantor's, or Maker's Name		
O Known O Introduced O ID Card/ID+KBA	Signer's, Grantor's, or Maker's mailing Address		
Exp.Date/Session ID	Brief description of the Document. If land is conveyed or charged, the name of the original grantee and the county where the land is located		
Meeting Type O Remote Online O In-Person Meeting	Introducer's, Witness's Name and Mailing address, identification method (Known/Introduced/ID card/ID+KBA [Exp.Date/Session ID])		
Document Type O Digital File O Paper Document	Notarization County	Document Date	Notarization Fee

Notarization Date	Signer's, Grantor's, or Maker's Name		
O Known O Introduced O ID Card/ID+KBA	Signer's, Grantor's, or Maker's mailing Address		
Exp.Date/Session ID	Brief description of the Document. If land is conveyed or charged, the name of the original grantee and the county where the land is located		
Meeting Type O Remote Online O In-Person Meeting	Introducer's, Witness's Name and Mailing address, identification method (Known/Introduced/ID card/ID+KBA [Exp.Date/Session ID])		
Document Type O Digital File O Paper Document	Notarization County	Document Date	Notarization Fee

Notarization Date	Signer's, Grantor's, or Maker's Name		
O Known O Introduced O ID Card/ID+KBA	Signer's, Grantor's, or Maker's mailing Address		
Exp.Date/Session ID	Brief description of the Document. If land is conveyed or charged, the name of the original grantee and the county where the land is located		
Meeting Type O Remote Online O In-Person Meeting	Introducer's, Witness's Name and Mailing address, identification method (Known/Introduced/ID card/ID+KBA [Exp.Date/Session ID])		
Document Type O Digital File O Paper Document	Notarization County	Document Date	Notarization Fee

Notarization Date	Signer's, Grantor's, or Maker's Name		
O Known O Introduced O ID Card/ID+KBA	Signer's, Grantor's, or Maker's mailing Address		
Exp.Date/Session ID	Brief description of the Document. If land is conveyed or charged, the name of the original grantee and the county where the land is located		
Meeting Type O Remote Online O In-Person Meeting	Introducer's, Witness's Name and Mailing address, identification method (Known/Introduced/ID card/ID+KBA [Exp.Date/Session ID])		
Document Type O Digital File O Paper Document	Notarization County	Document Date	Notarization Fee

Notarization Date	Signer's, Grantor's, or Maker's Name		
O Known O Introduced O ID Card/ID+KBA	Signer's, Grantor's, or Maker's mailing Address		
Exp.Date/Session ID	Brief description of the Document. If land is conveyed or charged, the name of the original grantee and the county where the land is located		
Meeting Type O Remote Online O In-Person Meeting	Introducer's, Witness's Name and Mailing address, identification method (Known/Introduced/ID card/ID+KBA [Exp.Date/Session ID])		
Document Type O Digital File O Paper Document	Notarization County	Document Date	Notarization Fee

Notarization Date	Signer's, Grantor's, or Maker's Name		
○ Known ○ Introduced ○ ID Card/ID+KBA	Signer's, Grantor's, or Maker's mailing Address Brief description of the Document. If land is conveyed or charged, the name of the original grantee and the county where the land is located		
Exp.Date/Session ID			
Meeting Type ○ Remote Online ○ In-Person Meeting	Introducer's, Witness's Name and Mailing address, identification method (Known/Introduced/ID card/ID+KBA [Exp.Date/Session ID])		
Document Type ○ Digital File ○ Paper Document	Notarization County	Document Date	Notarization Fee

Notarization Date	Signer's, Grantor's, or Maker's Name		
○ Known ○ Introduced ○ ID Card/ID+KBA	Signer's, Grantor's, or Maker's mailing Address Brief description of the Document. If land is conveyed or charged, the name of the original grantee and the county where the land is located		
Exp.Date/Session ID			
Meeting Type ○ Remote Online ○ In-Person Meeting	Introducer's, Witness's Name and Mailing address, identification method (Known/Introduced/ID card/ID+KBA [Exp.Date/Session ID])		
Document Type ○ Digital File ○ Paper Document	Notarization County	Document Date	Notarization Fee

Notarization Date	Signer's, Grantor's, or Maker's Name		
○ Known ○ Introduced ○ ID Card/ID+KBA	Signer's, Grantor's, or Maker's mailing Address Brief description of the Document. If land is conveyed or charged, the name of the original grantee and the county where the land is located		
Exp.Date/Session ID			
Meeting Type ○ Remote Online ○ In-Person Meeting	Introducer's, Witness's Name and Mailing address, identification method (Known/Introduced/ID card/ID+KBA [Exp.Date/Session ID])		
Document Type ○ Digital File ○ Paper Document	Notarization County	Document Date	Notarization Fee

Notarization Date	Signer's, Grantor's, or Maker's Name		
○ Known ○ Introduced ○ ID Card/ID+KBA	Signer's, Grantor's, or Maker's mailing Address Brief description of the Document. If land is conveyed or charged, the name of the original grantee and the county where the land is located		
Exp.Date/Session ID			
Meeting Type ○ Remote Online ○ In-Person Meeting	Introducer's, Witness's Name and Mailing address, identification method (Known/Introduced/ID card/ID+KBA [Exp.Date/Session ID])		
Document Type ○ Digital File ○ Paper Document	Notarization County	Document Date	Notarization Fee

Notarization Date	Signer's, Grantor's, or Maker's Name		
O Known O Introduced O ID Card/ID+KBA	Signer's, Grantor's, or Maker's mailing Address		
Exp.Date/Session ID	Brief description of the Document. If land is conveyed or charged, the name of the original grantee and the county where the land is located		
Meeting Type O Remote Online O In-Person Meeting	Introducer's, Witness's Name and Mailing address, identification method (Known/Introduced/ID card/ID+KBA [Exp.Date/Session ID])		
Document Type O Digital File O Paper Document	Notarization County	Document Date	Notarization Fee
Notarization Date	Signer's, Grantor's, or Maker's Name		
O Known O Introduced O ID Card/ID+KBA	Signer's, Grantor's, or Maker's mailing Address		
Exp.Date/Session ID	Brief description of the Document. If land is conveyed or charged, the name of the original grantee and the county where the land is located		
Meeting Type O Remote Online O In-Person Meeting	Introducer's, Witness's Name and Mailing address, identification method (Known/Introduced/ID card/ID+KBA [Exp.Date/Session ID])		
Document Type O Digital File O Paper Document	Notarization County	Document Date	Notarization Fee
Notarization Date	Signer's, Grantor's, or Maker's Name		
O Known O Introduced O ID Card/ID+KBA	Signer's, Grantor's, or Maker's mailing Address		
Exp.Date/Session ID	Brief description of the Document. If land is conveyed or charged, the name of the original grantee and the county where the land is located		
Meeting Type O Remote Online O In-Person Meeting	Introducer's, Witness's Name and Mailing address, identification method (Known/Introduced/ID card/ID+KBA [Exp.Date/Session ID])		
Document Type O Digital File O Paper Document	Notarization County	Document Date	Notarization Fee
Notarization Date	Signer's, Grantor's, or Maker's Name		
O Known O Introduced O ID Card/ID+KBA	Signer's, Grantor's, or Maker's mailing Address		
Exp.Date/Session ID	Brief description of the Document. If land is conveyed or charged, the name of the original grantee and the county where the land is located		
Meeting Type O Remote Online O In-Person Meeting	Introducer's, Witness's Name and Mailing address, identification method (Known/Introduced/ID card/ID+KBA [Exp.Date/Session ID])		
Document Type O Digital File O Paper Document	Notarization County	Document Date	Notarization Fee

Notarization Date	Signer's, Grantor's, or Maker's Name		
O Known O Introduced O ID Card/ID+KBA	Signer's, Grantor's, or Maker's mailing Address		
Exp.Date/Session ID	Brief description of the Document. If land is conveyed or charged, the name of the original grantee and the county where the land is located		
Meeting Type O Remote Online O In-Person Meeting	Introducer's, Witness's Name and Mailing address, identification method (Known/Introduced/ID card/ID+KBA [Exp.Date/Session ID])		
Document Type O Digital File O Paper Document	Notarization County	Document Date	Notarization Fee

Notarization Date	Signer's, Grantor's, or Maker's Name		
O Known O Introduced O ID Card/ID+KBA	Signer's, Grantor's, or Maker's mailing Address		
Exp.Date/Session ID	Brief description of the Document. If land is conveyed or charged, the name of the original grantee and the county where the land is located		
Meeting Type O Remote Online O In-Person Meeting	Introducer's, Witness's Name and Mailing address, identification method (Known/Introduced/ID card/ID+KBA [Exp.Date/Session ID])		
Document Type O Digital File O Paper Document	Notarization County	Document Date	Notarization Fee

Notarization Date	Signer's, Grantor's, or Maker's Name		
O Known O Introduced O ID Card/ID+KBA	Signer's, Grantor's, or Maker's mailing Address		
Exp.Date/Session ID	Brief description of the Document. If land is conveyed or charged, the name of the original grantee and the county where the land is located		
Meeting Type O Remote Online O In-Person Meeting	Introducer's, Witness's Name and Mailing address, identification method (Known/Introduced/ID card/ID+KBA [Exp.Date/Session ID])		
Document Type O Digital File O Paper Document	Notarization County	Document Date	Notarization Fee

Notarization Date	Signer's, Grantor's, or Maker's Name		
O Known O Introduced O ID Card/ID+KBA	Signer's, Grantor's, or Maker's mailing Address		
Exp.Date/Session ID	Brief description of the Document. If land is conveyed or charged, the name of the original grantee and the county where the land is located		
Meeting Type O Remote Online O In-Person Meeting	Introducer's, Witness's Name and Mailing address, identification method (Known/Introduced/ID card/ID+KBA [Exp.Date/Session ID])		
Document Type O Digital File O Paper Document	Notarization County	Document Date	Notarization Fee

Notarization Date	**Signer's, Grantor's, or Maker's Name**		
○ Known ○ Introduced ○ ID Card/ID+KBA	**Signer's, Grantor's, or Maker's mailing Address**		
	Brief description of the Document. If land is conveyed or charged, the name of the original grantee and the county where the land is located		
Exp.Date/Session ID			
Meeting Type ○ Remote Online ○ In-Person Meeting	Introducer's, Witness's Name and Mailing address, identification method (Known/Introduced/ID card/ID+KBA [Exp.Date/Session ID])		
Document Type ○ Digital File ○ Paper Document	**Notarization County**	**Document Date**	**Notarization Fee**

Notarization Date	Signer's, Grantor's, or Maker's Name		
○ Known ○ Introduced ○ ID Card/ID+KBA	**Signer's, Grantor's, or Maker's mailing Address**		
	Brief description of the Document. If land is conveyed or charged, the name of the original grantee and the county where the land is located		
Exp.Date/Session ID			
Meeting Type ○ Remote Online ○ In-Person Meeting	Introducer's, Witness's Name and Mailing address, identification method (Known/Introduced/ID card/ID+KBA [Exp.Date/Session ID])		
Document Type ○ Digital File ○ Paper Document	**Notarization County**	**Document Date**	**Notarization Fee**

Notarization Date	Signer's, Grantor's, or Maker's Name		
○ Known ○ Introduced ○ ID Card/ID+KBA	**Signer's, Grantor's, or Maker's mailing Address**		
	Brief description of the Document. If land is conveyed or charged, the name of the original grantee and the county where the land is located		
Exp.Date/Session ID			
Meeting Type ○ Remote Online ○ In-Person Meeting	Introducer's, Witness's Name and Mailing address, identification method (Known/Introduced/ID card/ID+KBA [Exp.Date/Session ID])		
Document Type ○ Digital File ○ Paper Document	**Notarization County**	**Document Date**	**Notarization Fee**

Notarization Date	Signer's, Grantor's, or Maker's Name		
○ Known ○ Introduced ○ ID Card/ID+KBA	**Signer's, Grantor's, or Maker's mailing Address**		
	Brief description of the Document. If land is conveyed or charged, the name of the original grantee and the county where the land is located		
Exp.Date/Session ID			
Meeting Type ○ Remote Online ○ In-Person Meeting	Introducer's, Witness's Name and Mailing address, identification method (Known/Introduced/ID card/ID+KBA [Exp.Date/Session ID])		
Document Type ○ Digital File ○ Paper Document	**Notarization County**	**Document Date**	**Notarization Fee**

Notarization Date	Signer's, Grantor's, or Maker's Name		
○ Known ○ Introduced ○ ID Card/ID+KBA	Signer's, Grantor's, or Maker's mailing Address		
Exp.Date/Session ID	Brief description of the Document. If land is conveyed or charged, the name of the original grantee and the county where the land is located		
Meeting Type ○ Remote Online ○ In-Person Meeting	Introducer's, Witness's Name and Mailing address, identification method (Known/Introduced/ID card/ID+KBA [Exp.Date/Session ID])		
Document Type ○ Digital File ○ Paper Document	Notarization County	Document Date	Notarization Fee

Notarization Date	Signer's, Grantor's, or Maker's Name		
○ Known ○ Introduced ○ ID Card/ID+KBA	Signer's, Grantor's, or Maker's mailing Address		
Exp.Date/Session ID	Brief description of the Document. If land is conveyed or charged, the name of the original grantee and the county where the land is located		
Meeting Type ○ Remote Online ○ In-Person Meeting	Introducer's, Witness's Name and Mailing address, identification method (Known/Introduced/ID card/ID+KBA [Exp.Date/Session ID])		
Document Type ○ Digital File ○ Paper Document	Notarization County	Document Date	Notarization Fee

Notarization Date	Signer's, Grantor's, or Maker's Name		
○ Known ○ Introduced ○ ID Card/ID+KBA	Signer's, Grantor's, or Maker's mailing Address		
Exp.Date/Session ID	Brief description of the Document. If land is conveyed or charged, the name of the original grantee and the county where the land is located		
Meeting Type ○ Remote Online ○ In-Person Meeting	Introducer's, Witness's Name and Mailing address, identification method (Known/Introduced/ID card/ID+KBA [Exp.Date/Session ID])		
Document Type ○ Digital File ○ Paper Document	Notarization County	Document Date	Notarization Fee

Notarization Date	Signer's, Grantor's, or Maker's Name		
○ Known ○ Introduced ○ ID Card/ID+KBA	Signer's, Grantor's, or Maker's mailing Address		
Exp.Date/Session ID	Brief description of the Document. If land is conveyed or charged, the name of the original grantee and the county where the land is located		
Meeting Type ○ Remote Online ○ In-Person Meeting	Introducer's, Witness's Name and Mailing address, identification method (Known/Introduced/ID card/ID+KBA [Exp.Date/Session ID])		
Document Type ○ Digital File ○ Paper Document	Notarization County	Document Date	Notarization Fee

Notarization Date	**Signer's, Grantor's, or Maker's Name**		
○ Known ○ Introduced ○ ID Card/ID+KBA	**Signer's, Grantor's, or Maker's mailing Address**		
Exp.Date/Session ID	Brief description of the Document. If land is conveyed or charged, the name of the original grantee and the county where the land is located		
Meeting Type ○ Remote Online ○ In-Person Meeting	Introducer's, Witness's Name and Mailing address, identification method (Known/Introduced/ID card/ID+KBA [Exp.Date/Session ID])		
Document Type ○ Digital File ○ Paper Document	**Notarization County**	**Document Date**	**Notarization Fee**

Notarization Date	Signer's, Grantor's, or Maker's Name		
○ Known ○ Introduced ○ ID Card/ID+KBA	**Signer's, Grantor's, or Maker's mailing Address**		
Exp.Date/Session ID	Brief description of the Document. If land is conveyed or charged, the name of the original grantee and the county where the land is located		
Meeting Type ○ Remote Online ○ In-Person Meeting	Introducer's, Witness's Name and Mailing address, identification method (Known/Introduced/ID card/ID+KBA [Exp.Date/Session ID])		
Document Type ○ Digital File ○ Paper Document	**Notarization County**	**Document Date**	**Notarization Fee**

Notarization Date	Signer's, Grantor's, or Maker's Name		
○ Known ○ Introduced ○ ID Card/ID+KBA	**Signer's, Grantor's, or Maker's mailing Address**		
Exp.Date/Session ID	Brief description of the Document. If land is conveyed or charged, the name of the original grantee and the county where the land is located		
Meeting Type ○ Remote Online ○ In-Person Meeting	Introducer's, Witness's Name and Mailing address, identification method (Known/Introduced/ID card/ID+KBA [Exp.Date/Session ID])		
Document Type ○ Digital File ○ Paper Document	**Notarization County**	**Document Date**	**Notarization Fee**

Notarization Date	Signer's, Grantor's, or Maker's Name		
○ Known ○ Introduced ○ ID Card/ID+KBA	**Signer's, Grantor's, or Maker's mailing Address**		
Exp.Date/Session ID	Brief description of the Document. If land is conveyed or charged, the name of the original grantee and the county where the land is located		
Meeting Type ○ Remote Online ○ In-Person Meeting	Introducer's, Witness's Name and Mailing address, identification method (Known/Introduced/ID card/ID+KBA [Exp.Date/Session ID])		
Document Type ○ Digital File ○ Paper Document	**Notarization County**	**Document Date**	**Notarization Fee**

Notarization Date	Signer's, Grantor's, or Maker's Name		
O Known O Introduced O ID Card/ID+KBA	Signer's, Grantor's, or Maker's mailing Address		
Exp.Date/Session ID	Brief description of the Document. If land is conveyed or charged, the name of the original grantee and the county where the land is located		
Meeting Type O Remote Online O In-Person Meeting	Introducer's, Witness's Name and Mailing address, identification method (Known/Introduced/ID card/ID+KBA [Exp.Date/Session ID])		
Document Type O Digital File O Paper Document	Notarization County	Document Date	Notarization Fee

Notarization Date	Signer's, Grantor's, or Maker's Name		
O Known O Introduced O ID Card/ID+KBA	Signer's, Grantor's, or Maker's mailing Address		
Exp.Date/Session ID	Brief description of the Document. If land is conveyed or charged, the name of the original grantee and the county where the land is located		
Meeting Type O Remote Online O In-Person Meeting	Introducer's, Witness's Name and Mailing address, identification method (Known/Introduced/ID card/ID+KBA [Exp.Date/Session ID])		
Document Type O Digital File O Paper Document	Notarization County	Document Date	Notarization Fee

Notarization Date	Signer's, Grantor's, or Maker's Name		
O Known O Introduced O ID Card/ID+KBA	Signer's, Grantor's, or Maker's mailing Address		
Exp.Date/Session ID	Brief description of the Document. If land is conveyed or charged, the name of the original grantee and the county where the land is located		
Meeting Type O Remote Online O In-Person Meeting	Introducer's, Witness's Name and Mailing address, identification method (Known/Introduced/ID card/ID+KBA [Exp.Date/Session ID])		
Document Type O Digital File O Paper Document	Notarization County	Document Date	Notarization Fee

Notarization Date	Signer's, Grantor's, or Maker's Name		
O Known O Introduced O ID Card/ID+KBA	Signer's, Grantor's, or Maker's mailing Address		
Exp.Date/Session ID	Brief description of the Document. If land is conveyed or charged, the name of the original grantee and the county where the land is located		
Meeting Type O Remote Online O In-Person Meeting	Introducer's, Witness's Name and Mailing address, identification method (Known/Introduced/ID card/ID+KBA [Exp.Date/Session ID])		
Document Type O Digital File O Paper Document	Notarization County	Document Date	Notarization Fee

Notarization Date	**Signer's, Grantor's, or Maker's Name**		
○ Known ○ Introduced	**Signer's, Grantor's, or Maker's mailing Address**		
○ ID Card/ID+KBA **Exp.Date/Session ID**	Brief description of the Document. If land is conveyed or charged, the name of the original grantee and the county where the land is located		
Meeting Type ○ Remote Online ○ In-Person Meeting	Introducer's, Witness's Name and Mailing address, identification method (Known/Introduced/ID card/ID+KBA [Exp.Date/Session ID])		
Document Type ○ Digital File ○ Paper Document	**Notarization County**	**Document Date**	**Notarization Fee**

Notarization Date	Signer's, Grantor's, or Maker's Name		
○ Known ○ Introduced	**Signer's, Grantor's, or Maker's mailing Address**		
○ ID Card/ID+KBA **Exp.Date/Session ID**	Brief description of the Document. If land is conveyed or charged, the name of the original grantee and the county where the land is located		
Meeting Type ○ Remote Online ○ In-Person Meeting	Introducer's, Witness's Name and Mailing address, identification method (Known/Introduced/ID card/ID+KBA [Exp.Date/Session ID])		
Document Type ○ Digital File ○ Paper Document	**Notarization County**	**Document Date**	**Notarization Fee**

Notarization Date	Signer's, Grantor's, or Maker's Name		
○ Known ○ Introduced	**Signer's, Grantor's, or Maker's mailing Address**		
○ ID Card/ID+KBA **Exp.Date/Session ID**	Brief description of the Document. If land is conveyed or charged, the name of the original grantee and the county where the land is located		
Meeting Type ○ Remote Online ○ In-Person Meeting	Introducer's, Witness's Name and Mailing address, identification method (Known/Introduced/ID card/ID+KBA [Exp.Date/Session ID])		
Document Type ○ Digital File ○ Paper Document	**Notarization County**	**Document Date**	**Notarization Fee**

Notarization Date	Signer's, Grantor's, or Maker's Name		
○ Known ○ Introduced	**Signer's, Grantor's, or Maker's mailing Address**		
○ ID Card/ID+KBA **Exp.Date/Session ID**	Brief description of the Document. If land is conveyed or charged, the name of the original grantee and the county where the land is located		
Meeting Type ○ Remote Online ○ In-Person Meeting	Introducer's, Witness's Name and Mailing address, identification method (Known/Introduced/ID card/ID+KBA [Exp.Date/Session ID])		
Document Type ○ Digital File ○ Paper Document	**Notarization County**	**Document Date**	**Notarization Fee**

Notarization Date | **Signer's, Grantor's, or Maker's Name**

○ Known
○ Introduced
○ ID Card/ID+KBA

Exp.Date/Session ID

Signer's, Grantor's, or Maker's mailing Address

Brief description of the Document. If land is conveyed or charged, the name of the original grantee and the county where the land is located

Meeting Type
○ Remote Online
○ In-Person Meeting

Introducer's, Witness's Name and Mailing address, identification method (Known/Introduced/ID card/ID+KBA [Exp.Date/Session ID])

Document Type
○ Digital File
○ Paper Document

Notarization County	**Document Date**	**Notarization Fee**

Notarization Date | Signer's, Grantor's, or Maker's Name

○ Known
○ Introduced
○ ID Card/ID+KBA

Exp.Date/Session ID

Signer's, Grantor's, or Maker's mailing Address

Brief description of the Document. If land is conveyed or charged, the name of the original grantee and the county where the land is located

Meeting Type
○ Remote Online
○ In-Person Meeting

Introducer's, Witness's Name and Mailing address, identification method (Known/Introduced/ID card/ID+KBA [Exp.Date/Session ID])

Document Type
○ Digital File
○ Paper Document

Notarization County	**Document Date**	**Notarization Fee**

Notarization Date | Signer's, Grantor's, or Maker's Name

○ Known
○ Introduced
○ ID Card/ID+KBA

Exp.Date/Session ID

Signer's, Grantor's, or Maker's mailing Address

Brief description of the Document. If land is conveyed or charged, the name of the original grantee and the county where the land is located

Meeting Type
○ Remote Online
○ In-Person Meeting

Introducer's, Witness's Name and Mailing address, identification method (Known/Introduced/ID card/ID+KBA [Exp.Date/Session ID])

Document Type
○ Digital File
○ Paper Document

Notarization County	**Document Date**	**Notarization Fee**

Notarization Date | Signer's, Grantor's, or Maker's Name

○ Known
○ Introduced
○ ID Card/ID+KBA

Exp.Date/Session ID

Signer's, Grantor's, or Maker's mailing Address

Brief description of the Document. If land is conveyed or charged, the name of the original grantee and the county where the land is located

Meeting Type
○ Remote Online
○ In-Person Meeting

Introducer's, Witness's Name and Mailing address, identification method (Known/Introduced/ID card/ID+KBA [Exp.Date/Session ID])

Document Type
○ Digital File
○ Paper Document

Notarization County	**Document Date**	**Notarization Fee**

Notarization Date	Signer's, Grantor's, or Maker's Name		
○ Known ○ Introduced ○ ID Card/ID+KBA	Signer's, Grantor's, or Maker's mailing Address		
Exp.Date/Session ID	Brief description of the Document. If land is conveyed or charged, the name of the original grantee and the county where the land is located		
Meeting Type ○ Remote Online ○ In-Person Meeting	Introducer's, Witness's Name and Mailing address, identification method (Known/Introduced/ID card/ID+KBA [Exp.Date/Session ID])		
Document Type ○ Digital File ○ Paper Document	Notarization County	Document Date	Notarization Fee

Notarization Date	Signer's, Grantor's, or Maker's Name		
○ Known ○ Introduced ○ ID Card/ID+KBA	Signer's, Grantor's, or Maker's mailing Address		
Exp.Date/Session ID	Brief description of the Document. If land is conveyed or charged, the name of the original grantee and the county where the land is located		
Meeting Type ○ Remote Online ○ In-Person Meeting	Introducer's, Witness's Name and Mailing address, identification method (Known/Introduced/ID card/ID+KBA [Exp.Date/Session ID])		
Document Type ○ Digital File ○ Paper Document	Notarization County	Document Date	Notarization Fee

Notarization Date	Signer's, Grantor's, or Maker's Name		
○ Known ○ Introduced ○ ID Card/ID+KBA	Signer's, Grantor's, or Maker's mailing Address		
Exp.Date/Session ID	Brief description of the Document. If land is conveyed or charged, the name of the original grantee and the county where the land is located		
Meeting Type ○ Remote Online ○ In-Person Meeting	Introducer's, Witness's Name and Mailing address, identification method (Known/Introduced/ID card/ID+KBA [Exp.Date/Session ID])		
Document Type ○ Digital File ○ Paper Document	Notarization County	Document Date	Notarization Fee

Notarization Date	Signer's, Grantor's, or Maker's Name		
○ Known ○ Introduced ○ ID Card/ID+KBA	Signer's, Grantor's, or Maker's mailing Address		
Exp.Date/Session ID	Brief description of the Document. If land is conveyed or charged, the name of the original grantee and the county where the land is located		
Meeting Type ○ Remote Online ○ In-Person Meeting	Introducer's, Witness's Name and Mailing address, identification method (Known/Introduced/ID card/ID+KBA [Exp.Date/Session ID])		
Document Type ○ Digital File ○ Paper Document	Notarization County	Document Date	Notarization Fee

Notarization Date	Signer's, Grantor's, or Maker's Name		
O Known O Introduced O ID Card/ID+KBA	Signer's, Grantor's, or Maker's mailing Address		
Exp.Date/Session ID	Brief description of the Document. If land is conveyed or charged, the name of the original grantee and the county where the land is located		
Meeting Type O Remote Online O In-Person Meeting	Introducer's, Witness's Name and Mailing address, identification method (Known/Introduced/ID card/ID+KBA [Exp.Date/Session ID])		
Document Type O Digital File O Paper Document	Notarization County	Document Date	Notarization Fee

Notarization Date	Signer's, Grantor's, or Maker's Name		
O Known O Introduced O ID Card/ID+KBA	Signer's, Grantor's, or Maker's mailing Address		
Exp.Date/Session ID	Brief description of the Document. If land is conveyed or charged, the name of the original grantee and the county where the land is located		
Meeting Type O Remote Online O In-Person Meeting	Introducer's, Witness's Name and Mailing address, identification method (Known/Introduced/ID card/ID+KBA [Exp.Date/Session ID])		
Document Type O Digital File O Paper Document	Notarization County	Document Date	Notarization Fee

Notarization Date	Signer's, Grantor's, or Maker's Name		
O Known O Introduced O ID Card/ID+KBA	Signer's, Grantor's, or Maker's mailing Address		
Exp.Date/Session ID	Brief description of the Document. If land is conveyed or charged, the name of the original grantee and the county where the land is located		
Meeting Type O Remote Online O In-Person Meeting	Introducer's, Witness's Name and Mailing address, identification method (Known/Introduced/ID card/ID+KBA [Exp.Date/Session ID])		
Document Type O Digital File O Paper Document	Notarization County	Document Date	Notarization Fee

Notarization Date	Signer's, Grantor's, or Maker's Name		
O Known O Introduced O ID Card/ID+KBA	Signer's, Grantor's, or Maker's mailing Address		
Exp.Date/Session ID	Brief description of the Document. If land is conveyed or charged, the name of the original grantee and the county where the land is located		
Meeting Type O Remote Online O In-Person Meeting	Introducer's, Witness's Name and Mailing address, identification method (Known/Introduced/ID card/ID+KBA [Exp.Date/Session ID])		
Document Type O Digital File O Paper Document	Notarization County	Document Date	Notarization Fee

Notarization Date	Signer's, Grantor's, or Maker's Name		
O Known O Introduced O ID Card/ID+KBA	Signer's, Grantor's, or Maker's mailing Address		
Exp.Date/Session ID	Brief description of the Document. If land is conveyed or charged, the name of the original grantee and the county where the land is located		
Meeting Type O Remote Online O In-Person Meeting	Introducer's, Witness's Name and Mailing address, identification method (Known/Introduced/ID card/ID+KBA [Exp.Date/Session ID])		
Document Type O Digital File O Paper Document	**Notarization County**	**Document Date**	**Notarization Fee**

Notarization Date	Signer's, Grantor's, or Maker's Name		
O Known O Introduced O ID Card/ID+KBA	Signer's, Grantor's, or Maker's mailing Address		
Exp.Date/Session ID	Brief description of the Document. If land is conveyed or charged, the name of the original grantee and the county where the land is located		
Meeting Type O Remote Online O In-Person Meeting	Introducer's, Witness's Name and Mailing address, identification method (Known/Introduced/ID card/ID+KBA [Exp.Date/Session ID])		
Document Type O Digital File O Paper Document	**Notarization County**	**Document Date**	**Notarization Fee**

Notarization Date	Signer's, Grantor's, or Maker's Name		
O Known O Introduced O ID Card/ID+KBA	Signer's, Grantor's, or Maker's mailing Address		
Exp.Date/Session ID	Brief description of the Document. If land is conveyed or charged, the name of the original grantee and the county where the land is located		
Meeting Type O Remote Online O In-Person Meeting	Introducer's, Witness's Name and Mailing address, identification method (Known/Introduced/ID card/ID+KBA [Exp.Date/Session ID])		
Document Type O Digital File O Paper Document	**Notarization County**	**Document Date**	**Notarization Fee**

Notarization Date	Signer's, Grantor's, or Maker's Name		
O Known O Introduced O ID Card/ID+KBA	Signer's, Grantor's, or Maker's mailing Address		
Exp.Date/Session ID	Brief description of the Document. If land is conveyed or charged, the name of the original grantee and the county where the land is located		
Meeting Type O Remote Online O In-Person Meeting	Introducer's, Witness's Name and Mailing address, identification method (Known/Introduced/ID card/ID+KBA [Exp.Date/Session ID])		
Document Type O Digital File O Paper Document	**Notarization County**	**Document Date**	**Notarization Fee**

Notarization Date

Signer's, Grantor's, or Maker's Name

- ○ Known
- ○ Introduced
- ○ ID Card/ID+KBA

Exp.Date/Session ID

Signer's, Grantor's, or Maker's mailing Address

Brief description of the Document. If land is conveyed or charged, the name of the original grantee and the county where the land is located

Meeting Type

- ○ Remote Online
- ○ In-Person Meeting

Introducer's, Witness's Name and Mailing address, identification method (Known/Introduced/ID card/ID+KBA [Exp.Date/Session ID])

Document Type

- ○ Digital File
- ○ Paper Document

Notarization County	Document Date	Notarization Fee

Notarization Date

Signer's, Grantor's, or Maker's Name

- ○ Known
- ○ Introduced
- ○ ID Card/ID+KBA

Exp.Date/Session ID

Signer's, Grantor's, or Maker's mailing Address

Brief description of the Document. If land is conveyed or charged, the name of the original grantee and the county where the land is located

Meeting Type

- ○ Remote Online
- ○ In-Person Meeting

Introducer's, Witness's Name and Mailing address, identification method (Known/Introduced/ID card/ID+KBA [Exp.Date/Session ID])

Document Type

- ○ Digital File
- ○ Paper Document

Notarization County	Document Date	Notarization Fee

Notarization Date

Signer's, Grantor's, or Maker's Name

- ○ Known
- ○ Introduced
- ○ ID Card/ID+KBA

Exp.Date/Session ID

Signer's, Grantor's, or Maker's mailing Address

Brief description of the Document. If land is conveyed or charged, the name of the original grantee and the county where the land is located

Meeting Type

- ○ Remote Online
- ○ In-Person Meeting

Introducer's, Witness's Name and Mailing address, identification method (Known/Introduced/ID card/ID+KBA [Exp.Date/Session ID])

Document Type

- ○ Digital File
- ○ Paper Document

Notarization County	Document Date	Notarization Fee

Notarization Date

Signer's, Grantor's, or Maker's Name

- ○ Known
- ○ Introduced
- ○ ID Card/ID+KBA

Exp.Date/Session ID

Signer's, Grantor's, or Maker's mailing Address

Brief description of the Document. If land is conveyed or charged, the name of the original grantee and the county where the land is located

Meeting Type

- ○ Remote Online
- ○ In-Person Meeting

Introducer's, Witness's Name and Mailing address, identification method (Known/Introduced/ID card/ID+KBA [Exp.Date/Session ID])

Document Type

- ○ Digital File
- ○ Paper Document

Notarization County	Document Date	Notarization Fee

Notarization Date | **Signer's, Grantor's, or Maker's Name**

O Known
O Introduced
O ID Card/ID+KBA

Signer's, Grantor's, or Maker's mailing Address

Brief description of the Document. If land is conveyed or charged, the name of the original grantee and the county where the land is located

Exp.Date/Session ID

Meeting Type
O Remote Online
O In-Person Meeting

Introducer's, Witness's Name and Mailing address, identification method (Known/Introduced/ID card/ID+KBA [Exp.Date/Session ID])

Document Type
O Digital File
O Paper Document

Notarization County	**Document Date**	**Notarization Fee**

Notarization Date | Signer's, Grantor's, or Maker's Name

O Known
O Introduced
O ID Card/ID+KBA

Signer's, Grantor's, or Maker's mailing Address

Brief description of the Document. If land is conveyed or charged, the name of the original grantee and the county where the land is located

Exp.Date/Session ID

Meeting Type
O Remote Online
O In-Person Meeting

Introducer's, Witness's Name and Mailing address, identification method (Known/Introduced/ID card/ID+KBA [Exp.Date/Session ID])

Document Type
O Digital File
O Paper Document

Notarization County	**Document Date**	**Notarization Fee**

Notarization Date | Signer's, Grantor's, or Maker's Name

O Known
O Introduced
O ID Card/ID+KBA

Signer's, Grantor's, or Maker's mailing Address

Brief description of the Document. If land is conveyed or charged, the name of the original grantee and the county where the land is located

Exp.Date/Session ID

Meeting Type
O Remote Online
O In-Person Meeting

Introducer's, Witness's Name and Mailing address, identification method (Known/Introduced/ID card/ID+KBA [Exp.Date/Session ID])

Document Type
O Digital File
O Paper Document

Notarization County	**Document Date**	**Notarization Fee**

Notarization Date | Signer's, Grantor's, or Maker's Name

O Known
O Introduced
O ID Card/ID+KBA

Signer's, Grantor's, or Maker's mailing Address

Brief description of the Document. If land is conveyed or charged, the name of the original grantee and the county where the land is located

Exp.Date/Session ID

Meeting Type
O Remote Online
O In-Person Meeting

Introducer's, Witness's Name and Mailing address, identification method (Known/Introduced/ID card/ID+KBA [Exp.Date/Session ID])

Document Type
O Digital File
O Paper Document

Notarization County	**Document Date**	**Notarization Fee**

Notarization Date	Signer's, Grantor's, or Maker's Name		
○ Known ○ Introduced ○ ID Card/ID+KBA	Signer's, Grantor's, or Maker's mailing Address		
Exp.Date/Session ID	Brief description of the Document. If land is conveyed or charged, the name of the original grantee and the county where the land is located		
Meeting Type ○ Remote Online ○ In-Person Meeting	Introducer's, Witness's Name and Mailing address, identification method (Known/Introduced/ID card/ID+KBA [Exp.Date/Session ID])		
Document Type ○ Digital File ○ Paper Document	Notarization County	Document Date	Notarization Fee

Notarization Date	Signer's, Grantor's, or Maker's Name		
○ Known ○ Introduced ○ ID Card/ID+KBA	Signer's, Grantor's, or Maker's mailing Address		
Exp.Date/Session ID	Brief description of the Document. If land is conveyed or charged, the name of the original grantee and the county where the land is located		
Meeting Type ○ Remote Online ○ In-Person Meeting	Introducer's, Witness's Name and Mailing address, identification method (Known/Introduced/ID card/ID+KBA [Exp.Date/Session ID])		
Document Type ○ Digital File ○ Paper Document	Notarization County	Document Date	Notarization Fee

Notarization Date	Signer's, Grantor's, or Maker's Name		
○ Known ○ Introduced ○ ID Card/ID+KBA	Signer's, Grantor's, or Maker's mailing Address		
Exp.Date/Session ID	Brief description of the Document. If land is conveyed or charged, the name of the original grantee and the county where the land is located		
Meeting Type ○ Remote Online ○ In-Person Meeting	Introducer's, Witness's Name and Mailing address, identification method (Known/Introduced/ID card/ID+KBA [Exp.Date/Session ID])		
Document Type ○ Digital File ○ Paper Document	Notarization County	Document Date	Notarization Fee

Notarization Date	Signer's, Grantor's, or Maker's Name		
○ Known ○ Introduced ○ ID Card/ID+KBA	Signer's, Grantor's, or Maker's mailing Address		
Exp.Date/Session ID	Brief description of the Document. If land is conveyed or charged, the name of the original grantee and the county where the land is located		
Meeting Type ○ Remote Online ○ In-Person Meeting	Introducer's, Witness's Name and Mailing address, identification method (Known/Introduced/ID card/ID+KBA [Exp.Date/Session ID])		
Document Type ○ Digital File ○ Paper Document	Notarization County	Document Date	Notarization Fee

Notarization Date	Signer's, Grantor's, or Maker's Name		
O Known O Introduced O ID Card/ID+KBA	Signer's, Grantor's, or Maker's mailing Address		
	Brief description of the Document. If land is conveyed or charged, the name of the original grantee and the county where the land is located		
Exp.Date/Session ID			
Meeting Type O Remote Online O In-Person Meeting	Introducer's, Witness's Name and Mailing address, identification method (Known/Introduced/ID card/ID+KBA [Exp.Date/Session ID])		
Document Type O Digital File O Paper Document	Notarization County	Document Date	Notarization Fee

Notarization Date	Signer's, Grantor's, or Maker's Name		
O Known O Introduced O ID Card/ID+KBA	Signer's, Grantor's, or Maker's mailing Address		
	Brief description of the Document. If land is conveyed or charged, the name of the original grantee and the county where the land is located		
Exp.Date/Session ID			
Meeting Type O Remote Online O In-Person Meeting	Introducer's, Witness's Name and Mailing address, identification method (Known/Introduced/ID card/ID+KBA [Exp.Date/Session ID])		
Document Type O Digital File O Paper Document	Notarization County	Document Date	Notarization Fee

Notarization Date	Signer's, Grantor's, or Maker's Name		
O Known O Introduced O ID Card/ID+KBA	Signer's, Grantor's, or Maker's mailing Address		
	Brief description of the Document. If land is conveyed or charged, the name of the original grantee and the county where the land is located		
Exp.Date/Session ID			
Meeting Type O Remote Online O In-Person Meeting	Introducer's, Witness's Name and Mailing address, identification method (Known/Introduced/ID card/ID+KBA [Exp.Date/Session ID])		
Document Type O Digital File O Paper Document	Notarization County	Document Date	Notarization Fee

Notarization Date	Signer's, Grantor's, or Maker's Name		
O Known O Introduced O ID Card/ID+KBA	Signer's, Grantor's, or Maker's mailing Address		
	Brief description of the Document. If land is conveyed or charged, the name of the original grantee and the county where the land is located		
Exp.Date/Session ID			
Meeting Type O Remote Online O In-Person Meeting	Introducer's, Witness's Name and Mailing address, identification method (Known/Introduced/ID card/ID+KBA [Exp.Date/Session ID])		
Document Type O Digital File O Paper Document	Notarization County	Document Date	Notarization Fee

Notarization Date | **Signer's, Grantor's, or Maker's Name**

- O Known
- O Introduced
- O ID Card/ID+KBA

Signer's, Grantor's, or Maker's mailing Address

Brief description of the Document. If land is conveyed or charged, the name of the original grantee and the county where the land is located

Exp.Date/Session ID

Meeting Type

- O Remote Online
- O In-Person Meeting

Introducer's, Witness's Name and Mailing address, identification method (Known/Introduced/ID card/ID+KBA [Exp.Date/Session ID])

Document Type

- O Digital File
- O Paper Document

Notarization County	Document Date	Notarization Fee

Notarization Date | Signer's, Grantor's, or Maker's Name

- O Known
- O Introduced
- O ID Card/ID+KBA

Signer's, Grantor's, or Maker's mailing Address

Brief description of the Document. If land is conveyed or charged, the name of the original grantee and the county where the land is located

Exp.Date/Session ID

Meeting Type

- O Remote Online
- O In-Person Meeting

Introducer's, Witness's Name and Mailing address, identification method (Known/Introduced/ID card/ID+KBA [Exp.Date/Session ID])

Document Type

- O Digital File
- O Paper Document

Notarization County	Document Date	Notarization Fee

Notarization Date | Signer's, Grantor's, or Maker's Name

- O Known
- O Introduced
- O ID Card/ID+KBA

Signer's, Grantor's, or Maker's mailing Address

Brief description of the Document. If land is conveyed or charged, the name of the original grantee and the county where the land is located

Exp.Date/Session ID

Meeting Type

- O Remote Online
- O In-Person Meeting

Introducer's, Witness's Name and Mailing address, identification method (Known/Introduced/ID card/ID+KBA [Exp.Date/Session ID])

Document Type

- O Digital File
- O Paper Document

Notarization County	Document Date	Notarization Fee

Notarization Date | Signer's, Grantor's, or Maker's Name

- O Known
- O Introduced
- O ID Card/ID+KBA

Signer's, Grantor's, or Maker's mailing Address

Brief description of the Document. If land is conveyed or charged, the name of the original grantee and the county where the land is located

Exp.Date/Session ID

Meeting Type

- O Remote Online
- O In-Person Meeting

Introducer's, Witness's Name and Mailing address, identification method (Known/Introduced/ID card/ID+KBA [Exp.Date/Session ID])

Document Type

- O Digital File
- O Paper Document

Notarization County	Document Date	Notarization Fee

Notarization Date	Signer's, Grantor's, or Maker's Name		
O Known O Introduced O ID Card/ID+KBA	Signer's, Grantor's, or Maker's mailing Address		
	Brief description of the Document. If land is conveyed or charged, the name of the original grantee and the county where the land is located		
Exp.Date/Session ID			
Meeting Type O Remote Online O In-Person Meeting	Introducer's, Witness's Name and Mailing address, identification method (Known/Introduced/ID card/ID+KBA [Exp.Date/Session ID])		
Document Type O Digital File O Paper Document	Notarization County	Document Date	Notarization Fee

Notarization Date	Signer's, Grantor's, or Maker's Name		
O Known O Introduced O ID Card/ID+KBA	Signer's, Grantor's, or Maker's mailing Address		
	Brief description of the Document. If land is conveyed or charged, the name of the original grantee and the county where the land is located		
Exp.Date/Session ID			
Meeting Type O Remote Online O In-Person Meeting	Introducer's, Witness's Name and Mailing address, identification method (Known/Introduced/ID card/ID+KBA [Exp.Date/Session ID])		
Document Type O Digital File O Paper Document	Notarization County	Document Date	Notarization Fee

Notarization Date	Signer's, Grantor's, or Maker's Name		
O Known O Introduced O ID Card/ID+KBA	Signer's, Grantor's, or Maker's mailing Address		
	Brief description of the Document. If land is conveyed or charged, the name of the original grantee and the county where the land is located		
Exp.Date/Session ID			
Meeting Type O Remote Online O In-Person Meeting	Introducer's, Witness's Name and Mailing address, identification method (Known/Introduced/ID card/ID+KBA [Exp.Date/Session ID])		
Document Type O Digital File O Paper Document	Notarization County	Document Date	Notarization Fee

Notarization Date	Signer's, Grantor's, or Maker's Name		
O Known O Introduced O ID Card/ID+KBA	Signer's, Grantor's, or Maker's mailing Address		
	Brief description of the Document. If land is conveyed or charged, the name of the original grantee and the county where the land is located		
Exp.Date/Session ID			
Meeting Type O Remote Online O In-Person Meeting	Introducer's, Witness's Name and Mailing address, identification method (Known/Introduced/ID card/ID+KBA [Exp.Date/Session ID])		
Document Type O Digital File O Paper Document	Notarization County	Document Date	Notarization Fee

Notarization Date	Signer's, Grantor's, or Maker's Name		
○ Known ○ Introduced	Signer's, Grantor's, or Maker's mailing Address		
○ ID Card/ID+KBA Exp.Date/Session ID	Brief description of the Document. If land is conveyed or charged, the name of the original grantee and the county where the land is located		
Meeting Type ○ Remote Online ○ In-Person Meeting	Introducer's, Witness's Name and Mailing address, identification method (Known/Introduced/ID card/ID+KBA [Exp.Date/Session ID])		
Document Type ○ Digital File ○ Paper Document	Notarization County	Document Date	Notarization Fee

Notarization Date	Signer's, Grantor's, or Maker's Name		
○ Known ○ Introduced	Signer's, Grantor's, or Maker's mailing Address		
○ ID Card/ID+KBA Exp.Date/Session ID	Brief description of the Document. If land is conveyed or charged, the name of the original grantee and the county where the land is located		
Meeting Type ○ Remote Online ○ In-Person Meeting	Introducer's, Witness's Name and Mailing address, identification method (Known/Introduced/ID card/ID+KBA [Exp.Date/Session ID])		
Document Type ○ Digital File ○ Paper Document	Notarization County	Document Date	Notarization Fee

Notarization Date	Signer's, Grantor's, or Maker's Name		
○ Known ○ Introduced	Signer's, Grantor's, or Maker's mailing Address		
○ ID Card/ID+KBA Exp.Date/Session ID	Brief description of the Document. If land is conveyed or charged, the name of the original grantee and the county where the land is located		
Meeting Type ○ Remote Online ○ In-Person Meeting	Introducer's, Witness's Name and Mailing address, identification method (Known/Introduced/ID card/ID+KBA [Exp.Date/Session ID])		
Document Type ○ Digital File ○ Paper Document	Notarization County	Document Date	Notarization Fee

Notarization Date	Signer's, Grantor's, or Maker's Name		
○ Known ○ Introduced	Signer's, Grantor's, or Maker's mailing Address		
○ ID Card/ID+KBA Exp.Date/Session ID	Brief description of the Document. If land is conveyed or charged, the name of the original grantee and the county where the land is located		
Meeting Type ○ Remote Online ○ In-Person Meeting	Introducer's, Witness's Name and Mailing address, identification method (Known/Introduced/ID card/ID+KBA [Exp.Date/Session ID])		
Document Type ○ Digital File ○ Paper Document	Notarization County	Document Date	Notarization Fee

Notarization Date | **Signer's, Grantor's, or Maker's Name**

○ Known
○ Introduced
○ ID Card/ID+KBA

Signer's, Grantor's, or Maker's mailing Address

Brief description of the Document. If land is conveyed or charged, the name of the original grantee and the county where the land is located

Exp.Date/Session ID

Meeting Type
○ Remote Online
○ In-Person Meeting

Introducer's, Witness's Name and Mailing address, identification method (Known/Introduced/ID card/ID+KBA [Exp.Date/Session ID])

Document Type
○ Digital File
○ Paper Document

Notarization County	**Document Date**	**Notarization Fee**

Notarization Date | Signer's, Grantor's, or Maker's Name

○ Known
○ Introduced
○ ID Card/ID+KBA

Signer's, Grantor's, or Maker's mailing Address

Brief description of the Document. If land is conveyed or charged, the name of the original grantee and the county where the land is located

Exp.Date/Session ID

Meeting Type
○ Remote Online
○ In-Person Meeting

Introducer's, Witness's Name and Mailing address, identification method (Known/Introduced/ID card/ID+KBA [Exp.Date/Session ID])

Document Type
○ Digital File
○ Paper Document

Notarization County	**Document Date**	**Notarization Fee**

Notarization Date | Signer's, Grantor's, or Maker's Name

○ Known
○ Introduced
○ ID Card/ID+KBA

Signer's, Grantor's, or Maker's mailing Address

Brief description of the Document. If land is conveyed or charged, the name of the original grantee and the county where the land is located

Exp.Date/Session ID

Meeting Type
○ Remote Online
○ In-Person Meeting

Introducer's, Witness's Name and Mailing address, identification method (Known/Introduced/ID card/ID+KBA [Exp.Date/Session ID])

Document Type
○ Digital File
○ Paper Document

Notarization County	**Document Date**	**Notarization Fee**

Notarization Date | Signer's, Grantor's, or Maker's Name

○ Known
○ Introduced
○ ID Card/ID+KBA

Signer's, Grantor's, or Maker's mailing Address

Brief description of the Document. If land is conveyed or charged, the name of the original grantee and the county where the land is located

Exp.Date/Session ID

Meeting Type
○ Remote Online
○ In-Person Meeting

Introducer's, Witness's Name and Mailing address, identification method (Known/Introduced/ID card/ID+KBA [Exp.Date/Session ID])

Document Type
○ Digital File
○ Paper Document

Notarization County	**Document Date**	**Notarization Fee**

Notarization Date	Signer's, Grantor's, or Maker's Name		
O Known O Introduced O ID Card/ID+KBA	Signer's, Grantor's, or Maker's mailing Address		
Exp.Date/Session ID	Brief description of the Document. If land is conveyed or charged, the name of the original grantee and the county where the land is located		
Meeting Type O Remote Online O In-Person Meeting	Introducer's, Witness's Name and Mailing address, identification method (Known/Introduced/ID card/ID+KBA [Exp.Date/Session ID])		
Document Type O Digital File O Paper Document	Notarization County	Document Date	Notarization Fee

Notarization Date	Signer's, Grantor's, or Maker's Name		
O Known O Introduced O ID Card/ID+KBA	Signer's, Grantor's, or Maker's mailing Address		
Exp.Date/Session ID	Brief description of the Document. If land is conveyed or charged, the name of the original grantee and the county where the land is located		
Meeting Type O Remote Online O In-Person Meeting	Introducer's, Witness's Name and Mailing address, identification method (Known/Introduced/ID card/ID+KBA [Exp.Date/Session ID])		
Document Type O Digital File O Paper Document	Notarization County	Document Date	Notarization Fee

Notarization Date	Signer's, Grantor's, or Maker's Name		
O Known O Introduced O ID Card/ID+KBA	Signer's, Grantor's, or Maker's mailing Address		
Exp.Date/Session ID	Brief description of the Document. If land is conveyed or charged, the name of the original grantee and the county where the land is located		
Meeting Type O Remote Online O In-Person Meeting	Introducer's, Witness's Name and Mailing address, identification method (Known/Introduced/ID card/ID+KBA [Exp.Date/Session ID])		
Document Type O Digital File O Paper Document	Notarization County	Document Date	Notarization Fee

Notarization Date	Signer's, Grantor's, or Maker's Name		
O Known O Introduced O ID Card/ID+KBA	Signer's, Grantor's, or Maker's mailing Address		
Exp.Date/Session ID	Brief description of the Document. If land is conveyed or charged, the name of the original grantee and the county where the land is located		
Meeting Type O Remote Online O In-Person Meeting	Introducer's, Witness's Name and Mailing address, identification method (Known/Introduced/ID card/ID+KBA [Exp.Date/Session ID])		
Document Type O Digital File O Paper Document	Notarization County	Document Date	Notarization Fee

Notarization Date	Signer's, Grantor's, or Maker's Name		
○ Known ○ Introduced ○ ID Card/ID+KBA	Signer's, Grantor's, or Maker's mailing Address		
Exp.Date/Session ID	Brief description of the Document. If land is conveyed or charged, the name of the original grantee and the county where the land is located		
Meeting Type ○ Remote Online ○ In-Person Meeting	Introducer's, Witness's Name and Mailing address, identification method (Known/Introduced/ID card/ID+KBA [Exp.Date/Session ID])		
Document Type ○ Digital File ○ Paper Document	Notarization County	Document Date	Notarization Fee

Notarization Date	Signer's, Grantor's, or Maker's Name		
○ Known ○ Introduced ○ ID Card/ID+KBA	Signer's, Grantor's, or Maker's mailing Address		
Exp.Date/Session ID	Brief description of the Document. If land is conveyed or charged, the name of the original grantee and the county where the land is located		
Meeting Type ○ Remote Online ○ In-Person Meeting	Introducer's, Witness's Name and Mailing address, identification method (Known/Introduced/ID card/ID+KBA [Exp.Date/Session ID])		
Document Type ○ Digital File ○ Paper Document	Notarization County	Document Date	Notarization Fee

Notarization Date	Signer's, Grantor's, or Maker's Name		
○ Known ○ Introduced ○ ID Card/ID+KBA	Signer's, Grantor's, or Maker's mailing Address		
Exp.Date/Session ID	Brief description of the Document. If land is conveyed or charged, the name of the original grantee and the county where the land is located		
Meeting Type ○ Remote Online ○ In-Person Meeting	Introducer's, Witness's Name and Mailing address, identification method (Known/Introduced/ID card/ID+KBA [Exp.Date/Session ID])		
Document Type ○ Digital File ○ Paper Document	Notarization County	Document Date	Notarization Fee

Notarization Date	Signer's, Grantor's, or Maker's Name		
○ Known ○ Introduced ○ ID Card/ID+KBA	Signer's, Grantor's, or Maker's mailing Address		
Exp.Date/Session ID	Brief description of the Document. If land is conveyed or charged, the name of the original grantee and the county where the land is located		
Meeting Type ○ Remote Online ○ In-Person Meeting	Introducer's, Witness's Name and Mailing address, identification method (Known/Introduced/ID card/ID+KBA [Exp.Date/Session ID])		
Document Type ○ Digital File ○ Paper Document	Notarization County	Document Date	Notarization Fee

Notarization Date	Signer's, Grantor's, or Maker's Name		
○ Known ○ Introduced ○ ID Card/ID+KBA	Signer's, Grantor's, or Maker's mailing Address		
Exp.Date/Session ID	Brief description of the Document. If land is conveyed or charged, the name of the original grantee and the county where the land is located		
Meeting Type ○ Remote Online ○ In-Person Meeting	Introducer's, Witness's Name and Mailing address, identification method (Known/Introduced/ID card/ID+KBA [Exp.Date/Session ID])		
Document Type ○ Digital File ○ Paper Document	**Notarization County**	**Document Date**	**Notarization Fee**

Notarization Date	Signer's, Grantor's, or Maker's Name		
○ Known ○ Introduced ○ ID Card/ID+KBA	Signer's, Grantor's, or Maker's mailing Address		
Exp.Date/Session ID	Brief description of the Document. If land is conveyed or charged, the name of the original grantee and the county where the land is located		
Meeting Type ○ Remote Online ○ In-Person Meeting	Introducer's, Witness's Name and Mailing address, identification method (Known/Introduced/ID card/ID+KBA [Exp.Date/Session ID])		
Document Type ○ Digital File ○ Paper Document	**Notarization County**	**Document Date**	**Notarization Fee**

Notarization Date	Signer's, Grantor's, or Maker's Name		
○ Known ○ Introduced ○ ID Card/ID+KBA	Signer's, Grantor's, or Maker's mailing Address		
Exp.Date/Session ID	Brief description of the Document. If land is conveyed or charged, the name of the original grantee and the county where the land is located		
Meeting Type ○ Remote Online ○ In-Person Meeting	Introducer's, Witness's Name and Mailing address, identification method (Known/Introduced/ID card/ID+KBA [Exp.Date/Session ID])		
Document Type ○ Digital File ○ Paper Document	**Notarization County**	**Document Date**	**Notarization Fee**

Notarization Date	Signer's, Grantor's, or Maker's Name		
○ Known ○ Introduced ○ ID Card/ID+KBA	Signer's, Grantor's, or Maker's mailing Address		
Exp.Date/Session ID	Brief description of the Document. If land is conveyed or charged, the name of the original grantee and the county where the land is located		
Meeting Type ○ Remote Online ○ In-Person Meeting	Introducer's, Witness's Name and Mailing address, identification method (Known/Introduced/ID card/ID+KBA [Exp.Date/Session ID])		
Document Type ○ Digital File ○ Paper Document	**Notarization County**	**Document Date**	**Notarization Fee**

Notarization Date | **Signer's, Grantor's, or Maker's Name**

○ Known
○ Introduced
○ ID Card/ID+KBA

Signer's, Grantor's, or Maker's mailing Address

Brief description of the Document. If land is conveyed or charged, the name of the original grantee and the county where the land is located

Exp.Date/Session ID

Meeting Type
○ Remote Online
○ In-Person Meeting

Introducer's, Witness's Name and Mailing address, identification method (Known/Introduced/ID card/ID+KBA [Exp.Date/Session ID])

Document Type
○ Digital File
○ Paper Document

Notarization County	**Document Date**	**Notarization Fee**

Notarization Date | Signer's, Grantor's, or Maker's Name

○ Known
○ Introduced
○ ID Card/ID+KBA

Signer's, Grantor's, or Maker's mailing Address

Brief description of the Document. If land is conveyed or charged, the name of the original grantee and the county where the land is located

Exp.Date/Session ID

Meeting Type
○ Remote Online
○ In-Person Meeting

Introducer's, Witness's Name and Mailing address, identification method (Known/Introduced/ID card/ID+KBA [Exp.Date/Session ID])

Document Type
○ Digital File
○ Paper Document

Notarization County	**Document Date**	**Notarization Fee**

Notarization Date | Signer's, Grantor's, or Maker's Name

○ Known
○ Introduced
○ ID Card/ID+KBA

Signer's, Grantor's, or Maker's mailing Address

Brief description of the Document. If land is conveyed or charged, the name of the original grantee and the county where the land is located

Exp.Date/Session ID

Meeting Type
○ Remote Online
○ In-Person Meeting

Introducer's, Witness's Name and Mailing address, identification method (Known/Introduced/ID card/ID+KBA [Exp.Date/Session ID])

Document Type
○ Digital File
○ Paper Document

Notarization County	**Document Date**	**Notarization Fee**

Notarization Date | Signer's, Grantor's, or Maker's Name

○ Known
○ Introduced
○ ID Card/ID+KBA

Signer's, Grantor's, or Maker's mailing Address

Brief description of the Document. If land is conveyed or charged, the name of the original grantee and the county where the land is located

Exp.Date/Session ID

Meeting Type
○ Remote Online
○ In-Person Meeting

Introducer's, Witness's Name and Mailing address, identification method (Known/Introduced/ID card/ID+KBA [Exp.Date/Session ID])

Document Type
○ Digital File
○ Paper Document

Notarization County	**Document Date**	**Notarization Fee**

Notarization Date	Signer's, Grantor's, or Maker's Name		
○ Known ○ Introduced ○ ID Card/ID+KBA	Signer's, Grantor's, or Maker's mailing Address		
	Brief description of the Document. If land is conveyed or charged, the name of the original grantee and the county where the land is located		
Exp.Date/Session ID			
Meeting Type ○ Remote Online ○ In-Person Meeting	Introducer's, Witness's Name and Mailing address, identification method (Known/Introduced/ID card/ID+KBA [Exp.Date/Session ID])		
Document Type ○ Digital File ○ Paper Document	Notarization County	Document Date	Notarization Fee

Notarization Date	Signer's, Grantor's, or Maker's Name		
○ Known ○ Introduced ○ ID Card/ID+KBA	Signer's, Grantor's, or Maker's mailing Address		
	Brief description of the Document. If land is conveyed or charged, the name of the original grantee and the county where the land is located		
Exp.Date/Session ID			
Meeting Type ○ Remote Online ○ In-Person Meeting	Introducer's, Witness's Name and Mailing address, identification method (Known/Introduced/ID card/ID+KBA [Exp.Date/Session ID])		
Document Type ○ Digital File ○ Paper Document	Notarization County	Document Date	Notarization Fee

Notarization Date	Signer's, Grantor's, or Maker's Name		
○ Known ○ Introduced ○ ID Card/ID+KBA	Signer's, Grantor's, or Maker's mailing Address		
	Brief description of the Document. If land is conveyed or charged, the name of the original grantee and the county where the land is located		
Exp.Date/Session ID			
Meeting Type ○ Remote Online ○ In-Person Meeting	Introducer's, Witness's Name and Mailing address, identification method (Known/Introduced/ID card/ID+KBA [Exp.Date/Session ID])		
Document Type ○ Digital File ○ Paper Document	Notarization County	Document Date	Notarization Fee

Notarization Date	Signer's, Grantor's, or Maker's Name		
○ Known ○ Introduced ○ ID Card/ID+KBA	Signer's, Grantor's, or Maker's mailing Address		
	Brief description of the Document. If land is conveyed or charged, the name of the original grantee and the county where the land is located		
Exp.Date/Session ID			
Meeting Type ○ Remote Online ○ In-Person Meeting	Introducer's, Witness's Name and Mailing address, identification method (Known/Introduced/ID card/ID+KBA [Exp.Date/Session ID])		
Document Type ○ Digital File ○ Paper Document	Notarization County	Document Date	Notarization Fee

Notarization Date	**Signer's, Grantor's, or Maker's Name**		
○ Known ○ Introduced ○ ID Card/ID+KBA	**Signer's, Grantor's, or Maker's mailing Address**		
Exp.Date/Session ID	Brief description of the Document. If land is conveyed or charged, the name of the original grantee and the county where the land is located		
Meeting Type ○ Remote Online ○ In-Person Meeting	Introducer's, Witness's Name and Mailing address, identification method (Known/Introduced/ID card/ID+KBA [Exp.Date/Session ID])		
Document Type ○ Digital File ○ Paper Document	**Notarization County**	**Document Date**	**Notarization Fee**

Notarization Date	Signer's, Grantor's, or Maker's Name		
○ Known ○ Introduced ○ ID Card/ID+KBA	**Signer's, Grantor's, or Maker's mailing Address**		
Exp.Date/Session ID	Brief description of the Document. If land is conveyed or charged, the name of the original grantee and the county where the land is located		
Meeting Type ○ Remote Online ○ In-Person Meeting	Introducer's, Witness's Name and Mailing address, identification method (Known/Introduced/ID card/ID+KBA [Exp.Date/Session ID])		
Document Type ○ Digital File ○ Paper Document	**Notarization County**	**Document Date**	**Notarization Fee**

Notarization Date	Signer's, Grantor's, or Maker's Name		
○ Known ○ Introduced ○ ID Card/ID+KBA	**Signer's, Grantor's, or Maker's mailing Address**		
Exp.Date/Session ID	Brief description of the Document. If land is conveyed or charged, the name of the original grantee and the county where the land is located		
Meeting Type ○ Remote Online ○ In-Person Meeting	Introducer's, Witness's Name and Mailing address, identification method (Known/Introduced/ID card/ID+KBA [Exp.Date/Session ID])		
Document Type ○ Digital File ○ Paper Document	**Notarization County**	**Document Date**	**Notarization Fee**

Notarization Date	Signer's, Grantor's, or Maker's Name		
○ Known ○ Introduced ○ ID Card/ID+KBA	**Signer's, Grantor's, or Maker's mailing Address**		
Exp.Date/Session ID	Brief description of the Document. If land is conveyed or charged, the name of the original grantee and the county where the land is located		
Meeting Type ○ Remote Online ○ In-Person Meeting	Introducer's, Witness's Name and Mailing address, identification method (Known/Introduced/ID card/ID+KBA [Exp.Date/Session ID])		
Document Type ○ Digital File ○ Paper Document	**Notarization County**	**Document Date**	**Notarization Fee**

Notarization Date	Signer's, Grantor's, or Maker's Name		
O Known O Introduced O ID Card/ID+KBA	Signer's, Grantor's, or Maker's mailing Address		
Exp.Date/Session ID	Brief description of the Document. If land is conveyed or charged, the name of the original grantee and the county where the land is located		
Meeting Type O Remote Online O In-Person Meeting	Introducer's, Witness's Name and Mailing address, identification method (Known/Introduced/ID card/ID+KBA [Exp.Date/Session ID])		
Document Type O Digital File O Paper Document	Notarization County	Document Date	Notarization Fee
Notarization Date	Signer's, Grantor's, or Maker's Name		
O Known O Introduced O ID Card/ID+KBA	Signer's, Grantor's, or Maker's mailing Address		
Exp.Date/Session ID	Brief description of the Document. If land is conveyed or charged, the name of the original grantee and the county where the land is located		
Meeting Type O Remote Online O In-Person Meeting	Introducer's, Witness's Name and Mailing address, identification method (Known/Introduced/ID card/ID+KBA [Exp.Date/Session ID])		
Document Type O Digital File O Paper Document	Notarization County	Document Date	Notarization Fee
Notarization Date	Signer's, Grantor's, or Maker's Name		
O Known O Introduced O ID Card/ID+KBA	Signer's, Grantor's, or Maker's mailing Address		
Exp.Date/Session ID	Brief description of the Document. If land is conveyed or charged, the name of the original grantee and the county where the land is located		
Meeting Type O Remote Online O In-Person Meeting	Introducer's, Witness's Name and Mailing address, identification method (Known/Introduced/ID card/ID+KBA [Exp.Date/Session ID])		
Document Type O Digital File O Paper Document	Notarization County	Document Date	Notarization Fee
Notarization Date	Signer's, Grantor's, or Maker's Name		
O Known O Introduced O ID Card/ID+KBA	Signer's, Grantor's, or Maker's mailing Address		
Exp.Date/Session ID	Brief description of the Document. If land is conveyed or charged, the name of the original grantee and the county where the land is located		
Meeting Type O Remote Online O In-Person Meeting	Introducer's, Witness's Name and Mailing address, identification method (Known/Introduced/ID card/ID+KBA [Exp.Date/Session ID])		
Document Type O Digital File O Paper Document	Notarization County	Document Date	Notarization Fee

Notarization Date	**Signer's, Grantor's, or Maker's Name**		
○ Known ○ Introduced ○ ID Card/ID+KBA	**Signer's, Grantor's, or Maker's mailing Address**		
Exp.Date/Session ID	Brief description of the Document. If land is conveyed or charged, the name of the original grantee and the county where the land is located		
Meeting Type ○ Remote Online ○ In-Person Meeting	Introducer's, Witness's Name and Mailing address, identification method (Known/Introduced/ID card/ID+KBA [Exp.Date/Session ID])		
Document Type ○ Digital File ○ Paper Document	**Notarization County**	**Document Date**	**Notarization Fee**

Notarization Date	Signer's, Grantor's, or Maker's Name		
○ Known ○ Introduced ○ ID Card/ID+KBA	**Signer's, Grantor's, or Maker's mailing Address**		
Exp.Date/Session ID	Brief description of the Document. If land is conveyed or charged, the name of the original grantee and the county where the land is located		
Meeting Type ○ Remote Online ○ In-Person Meeting	Introducer's, Witness's Name and Mailing address, identification method (Known/Introduced/ID card/ID+KBA [Exp.Date/Session ID])		
Document Type ○ Digital File ○ Paper Document	**Notarization County**	**Document Date**	**Notarization Fee**

Notarization Date	Signer's, Grantor's, or Maker's Name		
○ Known ○ Introduced ○ ID Card/ID+KBA	**Signer's, Grantor's, or Maker's mailing Address**		
Exp.Date/Session ID	Brief description of the Document. If land is conveyed or charged, the name of the original grantee and the county where the land is located		
Meeting Type ○ Remote Online ○ In-Person Meeting	Introducer's, Witness's Name and Mailing address, identification method (Known/Introduced/ID card/ID+KBA [Exp.Date/Session ID])		
Document Type ○ Digital File ○ Paper Document	**Notarization County**	**Document Date**	**Notarization Fee**

Notarization Date	Signer's, Grantor's, or Maker's Name		
○ Known ○ Introduced ○ ID Card/ID+KBA	**Signer's, Grantor's, or Maker's mailing Address**		
Exp.Date/Session ID	Brief description of the Document. If land is conveyed or charged, the name of the original grantee and the county where the land is located		
Meeting Type ○ Remote Online ○ In-Person Meeting	Introducer's, Witness's Name and Mailing address, identification method (Known/Introduced/ID card/ID+KBA [Exp.Date/Session ID])		
Document Type ○ Digital File ○ Paper Document	**Notarization County**	**Document Date**	**Notarization Fee**

Notarization Date	Signer's, Grantor's, or Maker's Name		
○ Known ○ Introduced ○ ID Card/ID+KBA	Signer's, Grantor's, or Maker's mailing Address		
Exp.Date/Session ID	Brief description of the Document. If land is conveyed or charged, the name of the original grantee and the county where the land is located		
Meeting Type ○ Remote Online ○ In-Person Meeting	Introducer's, Witness's Name and Mailing address, identification method (Known/Introduced/ID card/ID+KBA [Exp.Date/Session ID])		
Document Type ○ Digital File ○ Paper Document	Notarization County	Document Date	Notarization Fee

Notarization Date	Signer's, Grantor's, or Maker's Name		
○ Known ○ Introduced ○ ID Card/ID+KBA	Signer's, Grantor's, or Maker's mailing Address		
Exp.Date/Session ID	Brief description of the Document. If land is conveyed or charged, the name of the original grantee and the county where the land is located		
Meeting Type ○ Remote Online ○ In-Person Meeting	Introducer's, Witness's Name and Mailing address, identification method (Known/Introduced/ID card/ID+KBA [Exp.Date/Session ID])		
Document Type ○ Digital File ○ Paper Document	Notarization County	Document Date	Notarization Fee

Notarization Date	Signer's, Grantor's, or Maker's Name		
○ Known ○ Introduced ○ ID Card/ID+KBA	Signer's, Grantor's, or Maker's mailing Address		
Exp.Date/Session ID	Brief description of the Document. If land is conveyed or charged, the name of the original grantee and the county where the land is located		
Meeting Type ○ Remote Online ○ In-Person Meeting	Introducer's, Witness's Name and Mailing address, identification method (Known/Introduced/ID card/ID+KBA [Exp.Date/Session ID])		
Document Type ○ Digital File ○ Paper Document	Notarization County	Document Date	Notarization Fee

Notarization Date	Signer's, Grantor's, or Maker's Name		
○ Known ○ Introduced ○ ID Card/ID+KBA	Signer's, Grantor's, or Maker's mailing Address		
Exp.Date/Session ID	Brief description of the Document. If land is conveyed or charged, the name of the original grantee and the county where the land is located		
Meeting Type ○ Remote Online ○ In-Person Meeting	Introducer's, Witness's Name and Mailing address, identification method (Known/Introduced/ID card/ID+KBA [Exp.Date/Session ID])		
Document Type ○ Digital File ○ Paper Document	Notarization County	Document Date	Notarization Fee

Notarization Date

Signer's, Grantor's, or Maker's Name

○ Known
○ Introduced
○ ID Card/ID+KBA

Signer's, Grantor's, or Maker's mailing Address

Brief description of the Document. If land is conveyed or charged, the name of the original grantee and the county where the land is located

Exp.Date/Session ID

Meeting Type
○ Remote Online
○ In-Person Meeting

Introducer's, Witness's Name and Mailing address, identification method (Known/Introduced/ID card/ID+KBA [Exp.Date/Session ID])

Document Type
○ Digital File
○ Paper Document

Notarization County | **Document Date** | **Notarization Fee**

Notarization Date

Signer's, Grantor's, or Maker's Name

○ Known
○ Introduced
○ ID Card/ID+KBA

Signer's, Grantor's, or Maker's mailing Address

Brief description of the Document. If land is conveyed or charged, the name of the original grantee and the county where the land is located

Exp.Date/Session ID

Meeting Type
○ Remote Online
○ In-Person Meeting

Introducer's, Witness's Name and Mailing address, identification method (Known/Introduced/ID card/ID+KBA [Exp.Date/Session ID])

Document Type
○ Digital File
○ Paper Document

Notarization County | **Document Date** | **Notarization Fee**

Notarization Date

Signer's, Grantor's, or Maker's Name

○ Known
○ Introduced
○ ID Card/ID+KBA

Signer's, Grantor's, or Maker's mailing Address

Brief description of the Document. If land is conveyed or charged, the name of the original grantee and the county where the land is located

Exp.Date/Session ID

Meeting Type
○ Remote Online
○ In-Person Meeting

Introducer's, Witness's Name and Mailing address, identification method (Known/Introduced/ID card/ID+KBA [Exp.Date/Session ID])

Document Type
○ Digital File
○ Paper Document

Notarization County | **Document Date** | **Notarization Fee**

Notarization Date

Signer's, Grantor's, or Maker's Name

○ Known
○ Introduced
○ ID Card/ID+KBA

Signer's, Grantor's, or Maker's mailing Address

Brief description of the Document. If land is conveyed or charged, the name of the original grantee and the county where the land is located

Exp.Date/Session ID

Meeting Type
○ Remote Online
○ In-Person Meeting

Introducer's, Witness's Name and Mailing address, identification method (Known/Introduced/ID card/ID+KBA [Exp.Date/Session ID])

Document Type
○ Digital File
○ Paper Document

Notarization County | **Document Date** | **Notarization Fee**

Notarization Date	Signer's, Grantor's, or Maker's Name		
O Known O Introduced O ID Card/ID+KBA	**Signer's, Grantor's, or Maker's mailing Address**		
Exp.Date/Session ID	Brief description of the Document. If land is conveyed or charged, the name of the original grantee and the county where the land is located		
Meeting Type O Remote Online O In-Person Meeting	Introducer's, Witness's Name and Mailing address, identification method (Known/Introduced/ID card/ID+KBA [Exp.Date/Session ID])		
Document Type O Digital File O Paper Document	**Notarization County**	**Document Date**	**Notarization Fee**
Notarization Date	Signer's, Grantor's, or Maker's Name		
O Known O Introduced O ID Card/ID+KBA	**Signer's, Grantor's, or Maker's mailing Address**		
Exp.Date/Session ID	Brief description of the Document. If land is conveyed or charged, the name of the original grantee and the county where the land is located		
Meeting Type O Remote Online O In-Person Meeting	Introducer's, Witness's Name and Mailing address, identification method (Known/Introduced/ID card/ID+KBA [Exp.Date/Session ID])		
Document Type O Digital File O Paper Document	**Notarization County**	**Document Date**	**Notarization Fee**
Notarization Date	Signer's, Grantor's, or Maker's Name		
O Known O Introduced O ID Card/ID+KBA	**Signer's, Grantor's, or Maker's mailing Address**		
Exp.Date/Session ID	Brief description of the Document. If land is conveyed or charged, the name of the original grantee and the county where the land is located		
Meeting Type O Remote Online O In-Person Meeting	Introducer's, Witness's Name and Mailing address, identification method (Known/Introduced/ID card/ID+KBA [Exp.Date/Session ID])		
Document Type O Digital File O Paper Document	**Notarization County**	**Document Date**	**Notarization Fee**
Notarization Date	Signer's, Grantor's, or Maker's Name		
O Known O Introduced O ID Card/ID+KBA	**Signer's, Grantor's, or Maker's mailing Address**		
Exp.Date/Session ID	Brief description of the Document. If land is conveyed or charged, the name of the original grantee and the county where the land is located		
Meeting Type O Remote Online O In-Person Meeting	Introducer's, Witness's Name and Mailing address, identification method (Known/Introduced/ID card/ID+KBA [Exp.Date/Session ID])		
Document Type O Digital File O Paper Document	**Notarization County**	**Document Date**	**Notarization Fee**

Notarization Date	Signer's, Grantor's, or Maker's Name		
○ Known ○ Introduced ○ ID Card/ID+KBA	**Signer's, Grantor's, or Maker's mailing Address** Brief description of the Document. If land is conveyed or charged, the name of the original grantee and the county where the land is located		
Exp.Date/Session ID			
Meeting Type ○ Remote Online ○ In-Person Meeting	Introducer's, Witness's Name and Mailing address, identification method (Known/Introduced/ID card/ID+KBA [Exp.Date/Session ID])		
Document Type ○ Digital File ○ Paper Document	**Notarization County**	**Document Date**	**Notarization Fee**

Notarization Date	Signer's, Grantor's, or Maker's Name		
○ Known ○ Introduced ○ ID Card/ID+KBA	**Signer's, Grantor's, or Maker's mailing Address** Brief description of the Document. If land is conveyed or charged, the name of the original grantee and the county where the land is located		
Exp.Date/Session ID			
Meeting Type ○ Remote Online ○ In-Person Meeting	Introducer's, Witness's Name and Mailing address, identification method (Known/Introduced/ID card/ID+KBA [Exp.Date/Session ID])		
Document Type ○ Digital File ○ Paper Document	**Notarization County**	**Document Date**	**Notarization Fee**

Notarization Date	Signer's, Grantor's, or Maker's Name		
○ Known ○ Introduced ○ ID Card/ID+KBA	**Signer's, Grantor's, or Maker's mailing Address** Brief description of the Document. If land is conveyed or charged, the name of the original grantee and the county where the land is located		
Exp.Date/Session ID			
Meeting Type ○ Remote Online ○ In-Person Meeting	Introducer's, Witness's Name and Mailing address, identification method (Known/Introduced/ID card/ID+KBA [Exp.Date/Session ID])		
Document Type ○ Digital File ○ Paper Document	**Notarization County**	**Document Date**	**Notarization Fee**

Notarization Date	Signer's, Grantor's, or Maker's Name		
○ Known ○ Introduced ○ ID Card/ID+KBA	**Signer's, Grantor's, or Maker's mailing Address** Brief description of the Document. If land is conveyed or charged, the name of the original grantee and the county where the land is located		
Exp.Date/Session ID			
Meeting Type ○ Remote Online ○ In-Person Meeting	Introducer's, Witness's Name and Mailing address, identification method (Known/Introduced/ID card/ID+KBA [Exp.Date/Session ID])		
Document Type ○ Digital File ○ Paper Document	**Notarization County**	**Document Date**	**Notarization Fee**

Notarization Date	Signer's, Grantor's, or Maker's Name		
○ Known ○ Introduced ○ ID Card/ID+KBA	Signer's, Grantor's, or Maker's mailing Address		
Exp.Date/Session ID	Brief description of the Document. If land is conveyed or charged, the name of the original grantee and the county where the land is located		
Meeting Type ○ Remote Online ○ In-Person Meeting	Introducer's, Witness's Name and Mailing address, identification method (Known/Introduced/ID card/ID+KBA [Exp.Date/Session ID])		
Document Type ○ Digital File ○ Paper Document	Notarization County	Document Date	Notarization Fee

Notarization Date	Signer's, Grantor's, or Maker's Name		
○ Known ○ Introduced ○ ID Card/ID+KBA	Signer's, Grantor's, or Maker's mailing Address		
Exp.Date/Session ID	Brief description of the Document. If land is conveyed or charged, the name of the original grantee and the county where the land is located		
Meeting Type ○ Remote Online ○ In-Person Meeting	Introducer's, Witness's Name and Mailing address, identification method (Known/Introduced/ID card/ID+KBA [Exp.Date/Session ID])		
Document Type ○ Digital File ○ Paper Document	Notarization County	Document Date	Notarization Fee

Notarization Date	Signer's, Grantor's, or Maker's Name		
○ Known ○ Introduced ○ ID Card/ID+KBA	Signer's, Grantor's, or Maker's mailing Address		
Exp.Date/Session ID	Brief description of the Document. If land is conveyed or charged, the name of the original grantee and the county where the land is located		
Meeting Type ○ Remote Online ○ In-Person Meeting	Introducer's, Witness's Name and Mailing address, identification method (Known/Introduced/ID card/ID+KBA [Exp.Date/Session ID])		
Document Type ○ Digital File ○ Paper Document	Notarization County	Document Date	Notarization Fee

Notarization Date	Signer's, Grantor's, or Maker's Name		
○ Known ○ Introduced ○ ID Card/ID+KBA	Signer's, Grantor's, or Maker's mailing Address		
Exp.Date/Session ID	Brief description of the Document. If land is conveyed or charged, the name of the original grantee and the county where the land is located		
Meeting Type ○ Remote Online ○ In-Person Meeting	Introducer's, Witness's Name and Mailing address, identification method (Known/Introduced/ID card/ID+KBA [Exp.Date/Session ID])		
Document Type ○ Digital File ○ Paper Document	Notarization County	Document Date	Notarization Fee

Notarization Date

Signer's, Grantor's, or Maker's Name

○ Known
○ Introduced
○ ID Card/ID+KBA

Signer's, Grantor's, or Maker's mailing Address

Brief description of the Document. If land is conveyed or charged, the name of the original grantee and the county where the land is located

Exp.Date/Session ID

Meeting Type
○ Remote Online
○ In-Person Meeting

Introducer's, Witness's Name and Mailing address, identification method (Known/Introduced/ID card/ID+KBA [Exp.Date/Session ID])

Document Type
○ Digital File
○ Paper Document

Notarization County	**Document Date**	**Notarization Fee**

Notarization Date

Signer's, Grantor's, or Maker's Name

○ Known
○ Introduced
○ ID Card/ID+KBA

Signer's, Grantor's, or Maker's mailing Address

Brief description of the Document. If land is conveyed or charged, the name of the original grantee and the county where the land is located

Exp.Date/Session ID

Meeting Type
○ Remote Online
○ In-Person Meeting

Introducer's, Witness's Name and Mailing address, identification method (Known/Introduced/ID card/ID+KBA [Exp.Date/Session ID])

Document Type
○ Digital File
○ Paper Document

Notarization County	**Document Date**	**Notarization Fee**

Notarization Date

Signer's, Grantor's, or Maker's Name

○ Known
○ Introduced
○ ID Card/ID+KBA

Signer's, Grantor's, or Maker's mailing Address

Brief description of the Document. If land is conveyed or charged, the name of the original grantee and the county where the land is located

Exp.Date/Session ID

Meeting Type
○ Remote Online
○ In-Person Meeting

Introducer's, Witness's Name and Mailing address, identification method (Known/Introduced/ID card/ID+KBA [Exp.Date/Session ID])

Document Type
○ Digital File
○ Paper Document

Notarization County	**Document Date**	**Notarization Fee**

Notarization Date

Signer's, Grantor's, or Maker's Name

○ Known
○ Introduced
○ ID Card/ID+KBA

Signer's, Grantor's, or Maker's mailing Address

Brief description of the Document. If land is conveyed or charged, the name of the original grantee and the county where the land is located

Exp.Date/Session ID

Meeting Type
○ Remote Online
○ In-Person Meeting

Introducer's, Witness's Name and Mailing address, identification method (Known/Introduced/ID card/ID+KBA [Exp.Date/Session ID])

Document Type
○ Digital File
○ Paper Document

Notarization County	**Document Date**	**Notarization Fee**

Notarization Date	Signer's, Grantor's, or Maker's Name		
○ Known ○ Introduced ○ ID Card/ID+KBA	Signer's, Grantor's, or Maker's mailing Address		
Exp.Date/Session ID	Brief description of the Document. If land is conveyed or charged, the name of the original grantee and the county where the land is located		
Meeting Type ○ Remote Online ○ In-Person Meeting	Introducer's, Witness's Name and Mailing address, identification method (Known/Introduced/ID card/ID+KBA [Exp.Date/Session ID])		
Document Type ○ Digital File ○ Paper Document	Notarization County	Document Date	Notarization Fee

Notarization Date	Signer's, Grantor's, or Maker's Name		
○ Known ○ Introduced ○ ID Card/ID+KBA	Signer's, Grantor's, or Maker's mailing Address		
Exp.Date/Session ID	Brief description of the Document. If land is conveyed or charged, the name of the original grantee and the county where the land is located		
Meeting Type ○ Remote Online ○ In-Person Meeting	Introducer's, Witness's Name and Mailing address, identification method (Known/Introduced/ID card/ID+KBA [Exp.Date/Session ID])		
Document Type ○ Digital File ○ Paper Document	Notarization County	Document Date	Notarization Fee

Notarization Date	Signer's, Grantor's, or Maker's Name		
○ Known ○ Introduced ○ ID Card/ID+KBA	Signer's, Grantor's, or Maker's mailing Address		
Exp.Date/Session ID	Brief description of the Document. If land is conveyed or charged, the name of the original grantee and the county where the land is located		
Meeting Type ○ Remote Online ○ In-Person Meeting	Introducer's, Witness's Name and Mailing address, identification method (Known/Introduced/ID card/ID+KBA [Exp.Date/Session ID])		
Document Type ○ Digital File ○ Paper Document	Notarization County	Document Date	Notarization Fee

Notarization Date	Signer's, Grantor's, or Maker's Name		
○ Known ○ Introduced ○ ID Card/ID+KBA	Signer's, Grantor's, or Maker's mailing Address		
Exp.Date/Session ID	Brief description of the Document. If land is conveyed or charged, the name of the original grantee and the county where the land is located		
Meeting Type ○ Remote Online ○ In-Person Meeting	Introducer's, Witness's Name and Mailing address, identification method (Known/Introduced/ID card/ID+KBA [Exp.Date/Session ID])		
Document Type ○ Digital File ○ Paper Document	Notarization County	Document Date	Notarization Fee

Notarization Date	Signer's, Grantor's, or Maker's Name		
○ Known ○ Introduced ○ ID Card/ID+KBA	Signer's, Grantor's, or Maker's mailing Address		
Exp.Date/Session ID	Brief description of the Document. If land is conveyed or charged, the name of the original grantee and the county where the land is located		
Meeting Type ○ Remote Online ○ In-Person Meeting	Introducer's, Witness's Name and Mailing address, identification method (Known/Introduced/ID card/ID+KBA [Exp.Date/Session ID])		
Document Type ○ Digital File ○ Paper Document	Notarization County	Document Date	Notarization Fee

Notarization Date	Signer's, Grantor's, or Maker's Name		
○ Known ○ Introduced ○ ID Card/ID+KBA	Signer's, Grantor's, or Maker's mailing Address		
Exp.Date/Session ID	Brief description of the Document. If land is conveyed or charged, the name of the original grantee and the county where the land is located		
Meeting Type ○ Remote Online ○ In-Person Meeting	Introducer's, Witness's Name and Mailing address, identification method (Known/Introduced/ID card/ID+KBA [Exp.Date/Session ID])		
Document Type ○ Digital File ○ Paper Document	Notarization County	Document Date	Notarization Fee

Notarization Date	Signer's, Grantor's, or Maker's Name		
○ Known ○ Introduced ○ ID Card/ID+KBA	Signer's, Grantor's, or Maker's mailing Address		
Exp.Date/Session ID	Brief description of the Document. If land is conveyed or charged, the name of the original grantee and the county where the land is located		
Meeting Type ○ Remote Online ○ In-Person Meeting	Introducer's, Witness's Name and Mailing address, identification method (Known/Introduced/ID card/ID+KBA [Exp.Date/Session ID])		
Document Type ○ Digital File ○ Paper Document	Notarization County	Document Date	Notarization Fee

Notarization Date	Signer's, Grantor's, or Maker's Name		
○ Known ○ Introduced ○ ID Card/ID+KBA	Signer's, Grantor's, or Maker's mailing Address		
Exp.Date/Session ID	Brief description of the Document. If land is conveyed or charged, the name of the original grantee and the county where the land is located		
Meeting Type ○ Remote Online ○ In-Person Meeting	Introducer's, Witness's Name and Mailing address, identification method (Known/Introduced/ID card/ID+KBA [Exp.Date/Session ID])		
Document Type ○ Digital File ○ Paper Document	Notarization County	Document Date	Notarization Fee

Notarization Date	**Signer's, Grantor's, or Maker's Name**		
O Known O Introduced O ID Card/ID+KBA	**Signer's, Grantor's, or Maker's mailing Address**		
Exp.Date/Session ID	Brief description of the Document. If land is conveyed or charged, the name of the original grantee and the county where the land is located		
Meeting Type O Remote Online O In-Person Meeting	Introducer's, Witness's Name and Mailing address, identification method (Known/Introduced/ID card/ID+KBA [Exp.Date/Session ID])		
Document Type O Digital File O Paper Document	**Notarization County**	**Document Date**	**Notarization Fee**

Notarization Date	Signer's, Grantor's, or Maker's Name		
O Known O Introduced O ID Card/ID+KBA	**Signer's, Grantor's, or Maker's mailing Address**		
Exp.Date/Session ID	Brief description of the Document. If land is conveyed or charged, the name of the original grantee and the county where the land is located		
Meeting Type O Remote Online O In-Person Meeting	Introducer's, Witness's Name and Mailing address, identification method (Known/Introduced/ID card/ID+KBA [Exp.Date/Session ID])		
Document Type O Digital File O Paper Document	**Notarization County**	**Document Date**	**Notarization Fee**

Notarization Date	Signer's, Grantor's, or Maker's Name		
O Known O Introduced O ID Card/ID+KBA	**Signer's, Grantor's, or Maker's mailing Address**		
Exp.Date/Session ID	Brief description of the Document. If land is conveyed or charged, the name of the original grantee and the county where the land is located		
Meeting Type O Remote Online O In-Person Meeting	Introducer's, Witness's Name and Mailing address, identification method (Known/Introduced/ID card/ID+KBA [Exp.Date/Session ID])		
Document Type O Digital File O Paper Document	**Notarization County**	**Document Date**	**Notarization Fee**

Notarization Date	Signer's, Grantor's, or Maker's Name		
O Known O Introduced O ID Card/ID+KBA	**Signer's, Grantor's, or Maker's mailing Address**		
Exp.Date/Session ID	Brief description of the Document. If land is conveyed or charged, the name of the original grantee and the county where the land is located		
Meeting Type O Remote Online O In-Person Meeting	Introducer's, Witness's Name and Mailing address, identification method (Known/Introduced/ID card/ID+KBA [Exp.Date/Session ID])		
Document Type O Digital File O Paper Document	**Notarization County**	**Document Date**	**Notarization Fee**

Notarization Date	Signer's, Grantor's, or Maker's Name		
O Known O Introduced O ID Card/ID+KBA	Signer's, Grantor's, or Maker's mailing Address		
Exp.Date/Session ID	Brief description of the Document. If land is conveyed or charged, the name of the original grantee and the county where the land is located		
Meeting Type O Remote Online O In-Person Meeting	Introducer's, Witness's Name and Mailing address, identification method (Known/Introduced/ID card/ID+KBA [Exp.Date/Session ID])		
Document Type O Digital File O Paper Document	Notarization County	Document Date	Notarization Fee

Notarization Date	Signer's, Grantor's, or Maker's Name		
O Known O Introduced O ID Card/ID+KBA	Signer's, Grantor's, or Maker's mailing Address		
Exp.Date/Session ID	Brief description of the Document. If land is conveyed or charged, the name of the original grantee and the county where the land is located		
Meeting Type O Remote Online O In-Person Meeting	Introducer's, Witness's Name and Mailing address, identification method (Known/Introduced/ID card/ID+KBA [Exp.Date/Session ID])		
Document Type O Digital File O Paper Document	Notarization County	Document Date	Notarization Fee

Notarization Date	Signer's, Grantor's, or Maker's Name		
O Known O Introduced O ID Card/ID+KBA	Signer's, Grantor's, or Maker's mailing Address		
Exp.Date/Session ID	Brief description of the Document. If land is conveyed or charged, the name of the original grantee and the county where the land is located		
Meeting Type O Remote Online O In-Person Meeting	Introducer's, Witness's Name and Mailing address, identification method (Known/Introduced/ID card/ID+KBA [Exp.Date/Session ID])		
Document Type O Digital File O Paper Document	Notarization County	Document Date	Notarization Fee

Notarization Date	Signer's, Grantor's, or Maker's Name		
O Known O Introduced O ID Card/ID+KBA	Signer's, Grantor's, or Maker's mailing Address		
Exp.Date/Session ID	Brief description of the Document. If land is conveyed or charged, the name of the original grantee and the county where the land is located		
Meeting Type O Remote Online O In-Person Meeting	Introducer's, Witness's Name and Mailing address, identification method (Known/Introduced/ID card/ID+KBA [Exp.Date/Session ID])		
Document Type O Digital File O Paper Document	Notarization County	Document Date	Notarization Fee

Notarization Date	Signer's, Grantor's, or Maker's Name		
○ Known ○ Introduced ○ ID Card/ID+KBA	Signer's, Grantor's, or Maker's mailing Address		
Exp.Date/Session ID	Brief description of the Document. If land is conveyed or charged, the name of the original grantee and the county where the land is located		
Meeting Type ○ Remote Online ○ In-Person Meeting	Introducer's, Witness's Name and Mailing address, identification method (Known/Introduced/ID card/ID+KBA [Exp.Date/Session ID])		
Document Type ○ Digital File ○ Paper Document	Notarization County	Document Date	Notarization Fee

Notarization Date	Signer's, Grantor's, or Maker's Name		
○ Known ○ Introduced ○ ID Card/ID+KBA	Signer's, Grantor's, or Maker's mailing Address		
Exp.Date/Session ID	Brief description of the Document. If land is conveyed or charged, the name of the original grantee and the county where the land is located		
Meeting Type ○ Remote Online ○ In-Person Meeting	Introducer's, Witness's Name and Mailing address, identification method (Known/Introduced/ID card/ID+KBA [Exp.Date/Session ID])		
Document Type ○ Digital File ○ Paper Document	Notarization County	Document Date	Notarization Fee

Notarization Date	Signer's, Grantor's, or Maker's Name		
○ Known ○ Introduced ○ ID Card/ID+KBA	Signer's, Grantor's, or Maker's mailing Address		
Exp.Date/Session ID	Brief description of the Document. If land is conveyed or charged, the name of the original grantee and the county where the land is located		
Meeting Type ○ Remote Online ○ In-Person Meeting	Introducer's, Witness's Name and Mailing address, identification method (Known/Introduced/ID card/ID+KBA [Exp.Date/Session ID])		
Document Type ○ Digital File ○ Paper Document	Notarization County	Document Date	Notarization Fee

Notarization Date	Signer's, Grantor's, or Maker's Name		
○ Known ○ Introduced ○ ID Card/ID+KBA	Signer's, Grantor's, or Maker's mailing Address		
Exp.Date/Session ID	Brief description of the Document. If land is conveyed or charged, the name of the original grantee and the county where the land is located		
Meeting Type ○ Remote Online ○ In-Person Meeting	Introducer's, Witness's Name and Mailing address, identification method (Known/Introduced/ID card/ID+KBA [Exp.Date/Session ID])		
Document Type ○ Digital File ○ Paper Document	Notarization County	Document Date	Notarization Fee

Notarization Date	**Signer's, Grantor's, or Maker's Name**		
○ Known ○ Introduced ○ ID Card/ID+KBA	**Signer's, Grantor's, or Maker's mailing Address**		
Exp.Date/Session ID	Brief description of the Document. If land is conveyed or charged, the name of the original grantee and the county where the land is located		
Meeting Type ○ Remote Online ○ In-Person Meeting	Introducer's, Witness's Name and Mailing address, identification method (Known/Introduced/ID card/ID+KBA [Exp.Date/Session ID])		
Document Type ○ Digital File ○ Paper Document	**Notarization County**	**Document Date**	**Notarization Fee**

Notarization Date	Signer's, Grantor's, or Maker's Name		
○ Known ○ Introduced ○ ID Card/ID+KBA	**Signer's, Grantor's, or Maker's mailing Address**		
Exp.Date/Session ID	Brief description of the Document. If land is conveyed or charged, the name of the original grantee and the county where the land is located		
Meeting Type ○ Remote Online ○ In-Person Meeting	Introducer's, Witness's Name and Mailing address, identification method (Known/Introduced/ID card/ID+KBA [Exp.Date/Session ID])		
Document Type ○ Digital File ○ Paper Document	**Notarization County**	**Document Date**	**Notarization Fee**

Notarization Date	Signer's, Grantor's, or Maker's Name		
○ Known ○ Introduced ○ ID Card/ID+KBA	**Signer's, Grantor's, or Maker's mailing Address**		
Exp.Date/Session ID	Brief description of the Document. If land is conveyed or charged, the name of the original grantee and the county where the land is located		
Meeting Type ○ Remote Online ○ In-Person Meeting	Introducer's, Witness's Name and Mailing address, identification method (Known/Introduced/ID card/ID+KBA [Exp.Date/Session ID])		
Document Type ○ Digital File ○ Paper Document	**Notarization County**	**Document Date**	**Notarization Fee**

Notarization Date	Signer's, Grantor's, or Maker's Name		
○ Known ○ Introduced ○ ID Card/ID+KBA	**Signer's, Grantor's, or Maker's mailing Address**		
Exp.Date/Session ID	Brief description of the Document. If land is conveyed or charged, the name of the original grantee and the county where the land is located		
Meeting Type ○ Remote Online ○ In-Person Meeting	Introducer's, Witness's Name and Mailing address, identification method (Known/Introduced/ID card/ID+KBA [Exp.Date/Session ID])		
Document Type ○ Digital File ○ Paper Document	**Notarization County**	**Document Date**	**Notarization Fee**

Notarization Date	Signer's, Grantor's, or Maker's Name		
O Known O Introduced O ID Card/ID+KBA	Signer's, Grantor's, or Maker's mailing Address		
Exp.Date/Session ID	Brief description of the Document. If land is conveyed or charged, the name of the original grantee and the county where the land is located		
Meeting Type O Remote Online O In-Person Meeting	Introducer's, Witness's Name and Mailing address, identification method (Known/Introduced/ID card/ID+KBA [Exp.Date/Session ID])		
Document Type O Digital File O Paper Document	**Notarization County**	**Document Date**	**Notarization Fee**

Notarization Date	Signer's, Grantor's, or Maker's Name		
O Known O Introduced O ID Card/ID+KBA	Signer's, Grantor's, or Maker's mailing Address		
Exp.Date/Session ID	Brief description of the Document. If land is conveyed or charged, the name of the original grantee and the county where the land is located		
Meeting Type O Remote Online O In-Person Meeting	Introducer's, Witness's Name and Mailing address, identification method (Known/Introduced/ID card/ID+KBA [Exp.Date/Session ID])		
Document Type O Digital File O Paper Document	**Notarization County**	**Document Date**	**Notarization Fee**

Notarization Date	Signer's, Grantor's, or Maker's Name		
O Known O Introduced O ID Card/ID+KBA	Signer's, Grantor's, or Maker's mailing Address		
Exp.Date/Session ID	Brief description of the Document. If land is conveyed or charged, the name of the original grantee and the county where the land is located		
Meeting Type O Remote Online O In-Person Meeting	Introducer's, Witness's Name and Mailing address, identification method (Known/Introduced/ID card/ID+KBA [Exp.Date/Session ID])		
Document Type O Digital File O Paper Document	**Notarization County**	**Document Date**	**Notarization Fee**

Notarization Date	Signer's, Grantor's, or Maker's Name		
O Known O Introduced O ID Card/ID+KBA	Signer's, Grantor's, or Maker's mailing Address		
Exp.Date/Session ID	Brief description of the Document. If land is conveyed or charged, the name of the original grantee and the county where the land is located		
Meeting Type O Remote Online O In-Person Meeting	Introducer's, Witness's Name and Mailing address, identification method (Known/Introduced/ID card/ID+KBA [Exp.Date/Session ID])		
Document Type O Digital File O Paper Document	**Notarization County**	**Document Date**	**Notarization Fee**

Notarization Date	Signer's, Grantor's, or Maker's Name		
○ Known ○ Introduced ○ ID Card/ID+KBA	Signer's, Grantor's, or Maker's mailing Address		
Exp.Date/Session ID	Brief description of the Document. If land is conveyed or charged, the name of the original grantee and the county where the land is located		
Meeting Type ○ Remote Online ○ In-Person Meeting	Introducer's, Witness's Name and Mailing address, identification method (Known/Introduced/ID card/ID+KBA [Exp.Date/Session ID])		
Document Type ○ Digital File ○ Paper Document	Notarization County	Document Date	Notarization Fee

Notarization Date	Signer's, Grantor's, or Maker's Name		
○ Known ○ Introduced ○ ID Card/ID+KBA	Signer's, Grantor's, or Maker's mailing Address		
Exp.Date/Session ID	Brief description of the Document. If land is conveyed or charged, the name of the original grantee and the county where the land is located		
Meeting Type ○ Remote Online ○ In-Person Meeting	Introducer's, Witness's Name and Mailing address, identification method (Known/Introduced/ID card/ID+KBA [Exp.Date/Session ID])		
Document Type ○ Digital File ○ Paper Document	Notarization County	Document Date	Notarization Fee

Notarization Date	Signer's, Grantor's, or Maker's Name		
○ Known ○ Introduced ○ ID Card/ID+KBA	Signer's, Grantor's, or Maker's mailing Address		
Exp.Date/Session ID	Brief description of the Document. If land is conveyed or charged, the name of the original grantee and the county where the land is located		
Meeting Type ○ Remote Online ○ In-Person Meeting	Introducer's, Witness's Name and Mailing address, identification method (Known/Introduced/ID card/ID+KBA [Exp.Date/Session ID])		
Document Type ○ Digital File ○ Paper Document	Notarization County	Document Date	Notarization Fee

Notarization Date	Signer's, Grantor's, or Maker's Name		
○ Known ○ Introduced ○ ID Card/ID+KBA	Signer's, Grantor's, or Maker's mailing Address		
Exp.Date/Session ID	Brief description of the Document. If land is conveyed or charged, the name of the original grantee and the county where the land is located		
Meeting Type ○ Remote Online ○ In-Person Meeting	Introducer's, Witness's Name and Mailing address, identification method (Known/Introduced/ID card/ID+KBA [Exp.Date/Session ID])		
Document Type ○ Digital File ○ Paper Document	Notarization County	Document Date	Notarization Fee

Notarization Date	**Signer's, Grantor's, or Maker's Name**		
○ Known ○ Introduced ○ ID Card/ID+KBA	**Signer's, Grantor's, or Maker's mailing Address**		
Exp.Date/Session ID	Brief description of the Document. If land is conveyed or charged, the name of the original grantee and the county where the land is located		
Meeting Type ○ Remote Online ○ In-Person Meeting	Introducer's, Witness's Name and Mailing address, identification method (Known/Introduced/ID card/ID+KBA [Exp.Date/Session ID])		
Document Type ○ Digital File ○ Paper Document	**Notarization County**	**Document Date**	**Notarization Fee**

Notarization Date	Signer's, Grantor's, or Maker's Name		
○ Known ○ Introduced ○ ID Card/ID+KBA	**Signer's, Grantor's, or Maker's mailing Address**		
Exp.Date/Session ID	Brief description of the Document. If land is conveyed or charged, the name of the original grantee and the county where the land is located		
Meeting Type ○ Remote Online ○ In-Person Meeting	Introducer's, Witness's Name and Mailing address, identification method (Known/Introduced/ID card/ID+KBA [Exp.Date/Session ID])		
Document Type ○ Digital File ○ Paper Document	**Notarization County**	**Document Date**	**Notarization Fee**

Notarization Date	Signer's, Grantor's, or Maker's Name		
○ Known ○ Introduced ○ ID Card/ID+KBA	**Signer's, Grantor's, or Maker's mailing Address**		
Exp.Date/Session ID	Brief description of the Document. If land is conveyed or charged, the name of the original grantee and the county where the land is located		
Meeting Type ○ Remote Online ○ In-Person Meeting	Introducer's, Witness's Name and Mailing address, identification method (Known/Introduced/ID card/ID+KBA [Exp.Date/Session ID])		
Document Type ○ Digital File ○ Paper Document	**Notarization County**	**Document Date**	**Notarization Fee**

Notarization Date	Signer's, Grantor's, or Maker's Name		
○ Known ○ Introduced ○ ID Card/ID+KBA	**Signer's, Grantor's, or Maker's mailing Address**		
Exp.Date/Session ID	Brief description of the Document. If land is conveyed or charged, the name of the original grantee and the county where the land is located		
Meeting Type ○ Remote Online ○ In-Person Meeting	Introducer's, Witness's Name and Mailing address, identification method (Known/Introduced/ID card/ID+KBA [Exp.Date/Session ID])		
Document Type ○ Digital File ○ Paper Document	**Notarization County**	**Document Date**	**Notarization Fee**

Notarization Date	Signer's, Grantor's, or Maker's Name		
○ Known ○ Introduced ○ ID Card/ID+KBA	Signer's, Grantor's, or Maker's mailing Address		
Exp.Date/Session ID	Brief description of the Document. If land is conveyed or charged, the name of the original grantee and the county where the land is located		
Meeting Type ○ Remote Online ○ In-Person Meeting	Introducer's, Witness's Name and Mailing address, identification method (Known/Introduced/ID card/ID+KBA [Exp.Date/Session ID])		
Document Type ○ Digital File ○ Paper Document	Notarization County	Document Date	Notarization Fee

Notarization Date	Signer's, Grantor's, or Maker's Name		
○ Known ○ Introduced ○ ID Card/ID+KBA	Signer's, Grantor's, or Maker's mailing Address		
Exp.Date/Session ID	Brief description of the Document. If land is conveyed or charged, the name of the original grantee and the county where the land is located		
Meeting Type ○ Remote Online ○ In-Person Meeting	Introducer's, Witness's Name and Mailing address, identification method (Known/Introduced/ID card/ID+KBA [Exp.Date/Session ID])		
Document Type ○ Digital File ○ Paper Document	Notarization County	Document Date	Notarization Fee

Notarization Date	Signer's, Grantor's, or Maker's Name		
○ Known ○ Introduced ○ ID Card/ID+KBA	Signer's, Grantor's, or Maker's mailing Address		
Exp.Date/Session ID	Brief description of the Document. If land is conveyed or charged, the name of the original grantee and the county where the land is located		
Meeting Type ○ Remote Online ○ In-Person Meeting	Introducer's, Witness's Name and Mailing address, identification method (Known/Introduced/ID card/ID+KBA [Exp.Date/Session ID])		
Document Type ○ Digital File ○ Paper Document	Notarization County	Document Date	Notarization Fee

Notarization Date	Signer's, Grantor's, or Maker's Name		
○ Known ○ Introduced ○ ID Card/ID+KBA	Signer's, Grantor's, or Maker's mailing Address		
Exp.Date/Session ID	Brief description of the Document. If land is conveyed or charged, the name of the original grantee and the county where the land is located		
Meeting Type ○ Remote Online ○ In-Person Meeting	Introducer's, Witness's Name and Mailing address, identification method (Known/Introduced/ID card/ID+KBA [Exp.Date/Session ID])		
Document Type ○ Digital File ○ Paper Document	Notarization County	Document Date	Notarization Fee

Notarization Date	Signer's, Grantor's, or Maker's Name		
○ Known ○ Introduced ○ ID Card/ID+KBA	Signer's, Grantor's, or Maker's mailing Address		
Exp.Date/Session ID	Brief description of the Document. If land is conveyed or charged, the name of the original grantee and the county where the land is located		
Meeting Type ○ Remote Online ○ In-Person Meeting	Introducer's, Witness's Name and Mailing address, identification method (Known/Introduced/ID card/ID+KBA [Exp.Date/Session ID])		
Document Type ○ Digital File ○ Paper Document	Notarization County	Document Date	Notarization Fee

Notarization Date	Signer's, Grantor's, or Maker's Name		
○ Known ○ Introduced ○ ID Card/ID+KBA	Signer's, Grantor's, or Maker's mailing Address		
Exp.Date/Session ID	Brief description of the Document. If land is conveyed or charged, the name of the original grantee and the county where the land is located		
Meeting Type ○ Remote Online ○ In-Person Meeting	Introducer's, Witness's Name and Mailing address, identification method (Known/Introduced/ID card/ID+KBA [Exp.Date/Session ID])		
Document Type ○ Digital File ○ Paper Document	Notarization County	Document Date	Notarization Fee

Notarization Date	Signer's, Grantor's, or Maker's Name		
○ Known ○ Introduced ○ ID Card/ID+KBA	Signer's, Grantor's, or Maker's mailing Address		
Exp.Date/Session ID	Brief description of the Document. If land is conveyed or charged, the name of the original grantee and the county where the land is located		
Meeting Type ○ Remote Online ○ In-Person Meeting	Introducer's, Witness's Name and Mailing address, identification method (Known/Introduced/ID card/ID+KBA [Exp.Date/Session ID])		
Document Type ○ Digital File ○ Paper Document	Notarization County	Document Date	Notarization Fee

Notarization Date	Signer's, Grantor's, or Maker's Name		
○ Known ○ Introduced ○ ID Card/ID+KBA	Signer's, Grantor's, or Maker's mailing Address		
Exp.Date/Session ID	Brief description of the Document. If land is conveyed or charged, the name of the original grantee and the county where the land is located		
Meeting Type ○ Remote Online ○ In-Person Meeting	Introducer's, Witness's Name and Mailing address, identification method (Known/Introduced/ID card/ID+KBA [Exp.Date/Session ID])		
Document Type ○ Digital File ○ Paper Document	Notarization County	Document Date	Notarization Fee

Notarization Date | **Signer's, Grantor's, or Maker's Name**

○ Known
○ Introduced
○ ID Card/ID+KBA

Exp.Date/Session ID

Signer's, Grantor's, or Maker's mailing Address

Brief description of the Document. If land is conveyed or charged, the name of the original grantee and the county where the land is located

Meeting Type

○ Remote Online
○ In-Person Meeting

Introducer's, Witness's Name and Mailing address, identification method (Known/Introduced/ID card/ID+KBA [Exp.Date/Session ID])

Document Type

○ Digital File
○ Paper Document

Notarization County	**Document Date**	**Notarization Fee**

Notarization Date | Signer's, Grantor's, or Maker's Name

○ Known
○ Introduced
○ ID Card/ID+KBA

Exp.Date/Session ID

Signer's, Grantor's, or Maker's mailing Address

Brief description of the Document. If land is conveyed or charged, the name of the original grantee and the county where the land is located

Meeting Type

○ Remote Online
○ In-Person Meeting

Introducer's, Witness's Name and Mailing address, identification method (Known/Introduced/ID card/ID+KBA [Exp.Date/Session ID])

Document Type

○ Digital File
○ Paper Document

Notarization County	**Document Date**	**Notarization Fee**

Notarization Date | Signer's, Grantor's, or Maker's Name

○ Known
○ Introduced
○ ID Card/ID+KBA

Exp.Date/Session ID

Signer's, Grantor's, or Maker's mailing Address

Brief description of the Document. If land is conveyed or charged, the name of the original grantee and the county where the land is located

Meeting Type

○ Remote Online
○ In-Person Meeting

Introducer's, Witness's Name and Mailing address, identification method (Known/Introduced/ID card/ID+KBA [Exp.Date/Session ID])

Document Type

○ Digital File
○ Paper Document

Notarization County	**Document Date**	**Notarization Fee**

Notarization Date | Signer's, Grantor's, or Maker's Name

○ Known
○ Introduced
○ ID Card/ID+KBA

Exp.Date/Session ID

Signer's, Grantor's, or Maker's mailing Address

Brief description of the Document. If land is conveyed or charged, the name of the original grantee and the county where the land is located

Meeting Type

○ Remote Online
○ In-Person Meeting

Introducer's, Witness's Name and Mailing address, identification method (Known/Introduced/ID card/ID+KBA [Exp.Date/Session ID])

Document Type

○ Digital File
○ Paper Document

Notarization County	**Document Date**	**Notarization Fee**

Notarization Date	Signer's, Grantor's, or Maker's Name		
○ Known ○ Introduced ○ ID Card/ID+KBA	Signer's, Grantor's, or Maker's mailing Address		
Exp.Date/Session ID	Brief description of the Document. If land is conveyed or charged, the name of the original grantee and the county where the land is located		
Meeting Type ○ Remote Online ○ In-Person Meeting	Introducer's, Witness's Name and Mailing address, identification method (Known/Introduced/ID card/ID+KBA [Exp.Date/Session ID])		
Document Type ○ Digital File ○ Paper Document	Notarization County	Document Date	Notarization Fee

Notarization Date	Signer's, Grantor's, or Maker's Name		
○ Known ○ Introduced ○ ID Card/ID+KBA	Signer's, Grantor's, or Maker's mailing Address		
Exp.Date/Session ID	Brief description of the Document. If land is conveyed or charged, the name of the original grantee and the county where the land is located		
Meeting Type ○ Remote Online ○ In-Person Meeting	Introducer's, Witness's Name and Mailing address, identification method (Known/Introduced/ID card/ID+KBA [Exp.Date/Session ID])		
Document Type ○ Digital File ○ Paper Document	Notarization County	Document Date	Notarization Fee

Notarization Date	Signer's, Grantor's, or Maker's Name		
○ Known ○ Introduced ○ ID Card/ID+KBA	Signer's, Grantor's, or Maker's mailing Address		
Exp.Date/Session ID	Brief description of the Document. If land is conveyed or charged, the name of the original grantee and the county where the land is located		
Meeting Type ○ Remote Online ○ In-Person Meeting	Introducer's, Witness's Name and Mailing address, identification method (Known/Introduced/ID card/ID+KBA [Exp.Date/Session ID])		
Document Type ○ Digital File ○ Paper Document	Notarization County	Document Date	Notarization Fee

Notarization Date	Signer's, Grantor's, or Maker's Name		
○ Known ○ Introduced ○ ID Card/ID+KBA	Signer's, Grantor's, or Maker's mailing Address		
Exp.Date/Session ID	Brief description of the Document. If land is conveyed or charged, the name of the original grantee and the county where the land is located		
Meeting Type ○ Remote Online ○ In-Person Meeting	Introducer's, Witness's Name and Mailing address, identification method (Known/Introduced/ID card/ID+KBA [Exp.Date/Session ID])		
Document Type ○ Digital File ○ Paper Document	Notarization County	Document Date	Notarization Fee

Notarization Date	Signer's, Grantor's, or Maker's Name		
○ Known ○ Introduced ○ ID Card/ID+KBA	Signer's, Grantor's, or Maker's mailing Address		
Exp.Date/Session ID	Brief description of the Document. If land is conveyed or charged, the name of the original grantee and the county where the land is located		
Meeting Type ○ Remote Online ○ In-Person Meeting	Introducer's, Witness's Name and Mailing address, identification method (Known/Introduced/ID card/ID+KBA [Exp.Date/Session ID])		
Document Type ○ Digital File ○ Paper Document	Notarization County	Document Date	Notarization Fee

Notarization Date	Signer's, Grantor's, or Maker's Name		
○ Known ○ Introduced ○ ID Card/ID+KBA	Signer's, Grantor's, or Maker's mailing Address		
Exp.Date/Session ID	Brief description of the Document. If land is conveyed or charged, the name of the original grantee and the county where the land is located		
Meeting Type ○ Remote Online ○ In-Person Meeting	Introducer's, Witness's Name and Mailing address, identification method (Known/Introduced/ID card/ID+KBA [Exp.Date/Session ID])		
Document Type ○ Digital File ○ Paper Document	Notarization County	Document Date	Notarization Fee

Notarization Date	Signer's, Grantor's, or Maker's Name		
○ Known ○ Introduced ○ ID Card/ID+KBA	Signer's, Grantor's, or Maker's mailing Address		
Exp.Date/Session ID	Brief description of the Document. If land is conveyed or charged, the name of the original grantee and the county where the land is located		
Meeting Type ○ Remote Online ○ In-Person Meeting	Introducer's, Witness's Name and Mailing address, identification method (Known/Introduced/ID card/ID+KBA [Exp.Date/Session ID])		
Document Type ○ Digital File ○ Paper Document	Notarization County	Document Date	Notarization Fee

Notarization Date	Signer's, Grantor's, or Maker's Name		
○ Known ○ Introduced ○ ID Card/ID+KBA	Signer's, Grantor's, or Maker's mailing Address		
Exp.Date/Session ID	Brief description of the Document. If land is conveyed or charged, the name of the original grantee and the county where the land is located		
Meeting Type ○ Remote Online ○ In-Person Meeting	Introducer's, Witness's Name and Mailing address, identification method (Known/Introduced/ID card/ID+KBA [Exp.Date/Session ID])		
Document Type ○ Digital File ○ Paper Document	Notarization County	Document Date	Notarization Fee

Notarization Date	Signer's, Grantor's, or Maker's Name		
○ Known ○ Introduced ○ ID Card/ID+KBA	**Signer's, Grantor's, or Maker's mailing Address**		
Exp.Date/Session ID	Brief description of the Document. If land is conveyed or charged, the name of the original grantee and the county where the land is located		
Meeting Type ○ Remote Online ○ In-Person Meeting	Introducer's, Witness's Name and Mailing address, identification method (Known/Introduced/ID card/ID+KBA [Exp.Date/Session ID])		
Document Type ○ Digital File ○ Paper Document	**Notarization County**	**Document Date**	**Notarization Fee**

Notarization Date	Signer's, Grantor's, or Maker's Name		
○ Known ○ Introduced ○ ID Card/ID+KBA	**Signer's, Grantor's, or Maker's mailing Address**		
Exp.Date/Session ID	Brief description of the Document. If land is conveyed or charged, the name of the original grantee and the county where the land is located		
Meeting Type ○ Remote Online ○ In-Person Meeting	Introducer's, Witness's Name and Mailing address, identification method (Known/Introduced/ID card/ID+KBA [Exp.Date/Session ID])		
Document Type ○ Digital File ○ Paper Document	**Notarization County**	**Document Date**	**Notarization Fee**

Notarization Date	Signer's, Grantor's, or Maker's Name		
○ Known ○ Introduced ○ ID Card/ID+KBA	**Signer's, Grantor's, or Maker's mailing Address**		
Exp.Date/Session ID	Brief description of the Document. If land is conveyed or charged, the name of the original grantee and the county where the land is located		
Meeting Type ○ Remote Online ○ In-Person Meeting	Introducer's, Witness's Name and Mailing address, identification method (Known/Introduced/ID card/ID+KBA [Exp.Date/Session ID])		
Document Type ○ Digital File ○ Paper Document	**Notarization County**	**Document Date**	**Notarization Fee**

Notarization Date	Signer's, Grantor's, or Maker's Name		
○ Known ○ Introduced ○ ID Card/ID+KBA	**Signer's, Grantor's, or Maker's mailing Address**		
Exp.Date/Session ID	Brief description of the Document. If land is conveyed or charged, the name of the original grantee and the county where the land is located		
Meeting Type ○ Remote Online ○ In-Person Meeting	Introducer's, Witness's Name and Mailing address, identification method (Known/Introduced/ID card/ID+KBA [Exp.Date/Session ID])		
Document Type ○ Digital File ○ Paper Document	**Notarization County**	**Document Date**	**Notarization Fee**

Notarization Date | **Signer's, Grantor's, or Maker's Name**

○ Known
○ Introduced
○ ID Card/ID+KBA

Signer's, Grantor's, or Maker's mailing Address

Brief description of the Document. If land is conveyed or charged, the name of the original grantee and the county where the land is located

Exp.Date/Session ID

Meeting Type
○ Remote Online
○ In-Person Meeting

Introducer's, Witness's Name and Mailing address, identification method (Known/Introduced/ID card/ID+KBA [Exp.Date/Session ID])

Document Type
○ Digital File
○ Paper Document

Notarization County	**Document Date**	**Notarization Fee**

Notarization Date | Signer's, Grantor's, or Maker's Name

○ Known
○ Introduced
○ ID Card/ID+KBA

Signer's, Grantor's, or Maker's mailing Address

Brief description of the Document. If land is conveyed or charged, the name of the original grantee and the county where the land is located

Exp.Date/Session ID

Meeting Type
○ Remote Online
○ In-Person Meeting

Introducer's, Witness's Name and Mailing address, identification method (Known/Introduced/ID card/ID+KBA [Exp.Date/Session ID])

Document Type
○ Digital File
○ Paper Document

Notarization County	**Document Date**	**Notarization Fee**

Notarization Date | Signer's, Grantor's, or Maker's Name

○ Known
○ Introduced
○ ID Card/ID+KBA

Signer's, Grantor's, or Maker's mailing Address

Brief description of the Document. If land is conveyed or charged, the name of the original grantee and the county where the land is located

Exp.Date/Session ID

Meeting Type
○ Remote Online
○ In-Person Meeting

Introducer's, Witness's Name and Mailing address, identification method (Known/Introduced/ID card/ID+KBA [Exp.Date/Session ID])

Document Type
○ Digital File
○ Paper Document

Notarization County	**Document Date**	**Notarization Fee**

Notarization Date | Signer's, Grantor's, or Maker's Name

○ Known
○ Introduced
○ ID Card/ID+KBA

Signer's, Grantor's, or Maker's mailing Address

Brief description of the Document. If land is conveyed or charged, the name of the original grantee and the county where the land is located

Exp.Date/Session ID

Meeting Type
○ Remote Online
○ In-Person Meeting

Introducer's, Witness's Name and Mailing address, identification method (Known/Introduced/ID card/ID+KBA [Exp.Date/Session ID])

Document Type
○ Digital File
○ Paper Document

Notarization County	**Document Date**	**Notarization Fee**

Notarization Date	Signer's, Grantor's, or Maker's Name		
○ Known ○ Introduced ○ ID Card/ID+KBA	Signer's, Grantor's, or Maker's mailing Address		
Exp.Date/Session ID	Brief description of the Document. If land is conveyed or charged, the name of the original grantee and the county where the land is located		
Meeting Type ○ Remote Online ○ In-Person Meeting	Introducer's, Witness's Name and Mailing address, identification method (Known/Introduced/ID card/ID+KBA [Exp.Date/Session ID])		
Document Type ○ Digital File ○ Paper Document	Notarization County	Document Date	Notarization Fee

Notarization Date	Signer's, Grantor's, or Maker's Name		
○ Known ○ Introduced ○ ID Card/ID+KBA	Signer's, Grantor's, or Maker's mailing Address		
Exp.Date/Session ID	Brief description of the Document. If land is conveyed or charged, the name of the original grantee and the county where the land is located		
Meeting Type ○ Remote Online ○ In-Person Meeting	Introducer's, Witness's Name and Mailing address, identification method (Known/Introduced/ID card/ID+KBA [Exp.Date/Session ID])		
Document Type ○ Digital File ○ Paper Document	Notarization County	Document Date	Notarization Fee

Notarization Date	Signer's, Grantor's, or Maker's Name		
○ Known ○ Introduced ○ ID Card/ID+KBA	Signer's, Grantor's, or Maker's mailing Address		
Exp.Date/Session ID	Brief description of the Document. If land is conveyed or charged, the name of the original grantee and the county where the land is located		
Meeting Type ○ Remote Online ○ In-Person Meeting	Introducer's, Witness's Name and Mailing address, identification method (Known/Introduced/ID card/ID+KBA [Exp.Date/Session ID])		
Document Type ○ Digital File ○ Paper Document	Notarization County	Document Date	Notarization Fee

Notarization Date	Signer's, Grantor's, or Maker's Name		
○ Known ○ Introduced ○ ID Card/ID+KBA	Signer's, Grantor's, or Maker's mailing Address		
Exp.Date/Session ID	Brief description of the Document. If land is conveyed or charged, the name of the original grantee and the county where the land is located		
Meeting Type ○ Remote Online ○ In-Person Meeting	Introducer's, Witness's Name and Mailing address, identification method (Known/Introduced/ID card/ID+KBA [Exp.Date/Session ID])		
Document Type ○ Digital File ○ Paper Document	Notarization County	Document Date	Notarization Fee

Notarization Date	Signer's, Grantor's, or Maker's Name		
○ Known ○ Introduced ○ ID Card/ID+KBA	Signer's, Grantor's, or Maker's mailing Address		
Exp.Date/Session ID	Brief description of the Document. If land is conveyed or charged, the name of the original grantee and the county where the land is located		
Meeting Type ○ Remote Online ○ In-Person Meeting	Introducer's, Witness's Name and Mailing address, identification method (Known/Introduced/ID card/ID+KBA [Exp.Date/Session ID])		
Document Type ○ Digital File ○ Paper Document	Notarization County	Document Date	Notarization Fee

Notarization Date	Signer's, Grantor's, or Maker's Name		
○ Known ○ Introduced ○ ID Card/ID+KBA	Signer's, Grantor's, or Maker's mailing Address		
Exp.Date/Session ID	Brief description of the Document. If land is conveyed or charged, the name of the original grantee and the county where the land is located		
Meeting Type ○ Remote Online ○ In-Person Meeting	Introducer's, Witness's Name and Mailing address, identification method (Known/Introduced/ID card/ID+KBA [Exp.Date/Session ID])		
Document Type ○ Digital File ○ Paper Document	Notarization County	Document Date	Notarization Fee

Notarization Date	Signer's, Grantor's, or Maker's Name		
○ Known ○ Introduced ○ ID Card/ID+KBA	Signer's, Grantor's, or Maker's mailing Address		
Exp.Date/Session ID	Brief description of the Document. If land is conveyed or charged, the name of the original grantee and the county where the land is located		
Meeting Type ○ Remote Online ○ In-Person Meeting	Introducer's, Witness's Name and Mailing address, identification method (Known/Introduced/ID card/ID+KBA [Exp.Date/Session ID])		
Document Type ○ Digital File ○ Paper Document	Notarization County	Document Date	Notarization Fee

Notarization Date	Signer's, Grantor's, or Maker's Name		
○ Known ○ Introduced ○ ID Card/ID+KBA	Signer's, Grantor's, or Maker's mailing Address		
Exp.Date/Session ID	Brief description of the Document. If land is conveyed or charged, the name of the original grantee and the county where the land is located		
Meeting Type ○ Remote Online ○ In-Person Meeting	Introducer's, Witness's Name and Mailing address, identification method (Known/Introduced/ID card/ID+KBA [Exp.Date/Session ID])		
Document Type ○ Digital File ○ Paper Document	Notarization County	Document Date	Notarization Fee

Notarization Date	Signer's, Grantor's, or Maker's Name		
O Known O Introduced O ID Card/ID+KBA	Signer's, Grantor's, or Maker's mailing Address		
Exp.Date/Session ID	Brief description of the Document. If land is conveyed or charged, the name of the original grantee and the county where the land is located		
Meeting Type O Remote Online O In-Person Meeting	Introducer's, Witness's Name and Mailing address, identification method (Known/Introduced/ID card/ID+KBA [Exp.Date/Session ID])		
Document Type O Digital File O Paper Document	Notarization County	Document Date	Notarization Fee

Notarization Date	Signer's, Grantor's, or Maker's Name		
O Known O Introduced O ID Card/ID+KBA	Signer's, Grantor's, or Maker's mailing Address		
Exp.Date/Session ID	Brief description of the Document. If land is conveyed or charged, the name of the original grantee and the county where the land is located		
Meeting Type O Remote Online O In-Person Meeting	Introducer's, Witness's Name and Mailing address, identification method (Known/Introduced/ID card/ID+KBA [Exp.Date/Session ID])		
Document Type O Digital File O Paper Document	Notarization County	Document Date	Notarization Fee

Notarization Date	Signer's, Grantor's, or Maker's Name		
O Known O Introduced O ID Card/ID+KBA	Signer's, Grantor's, or Maker's mailing Address		
Exp.Date/Session ID	Brief description of the Document. If land is conveyed or charged, the name of the original grantee and the county where the land is located		
Meeting Type O Remote Online O In-Person Meeting	Introducer's, Witness's Name and Mailing address, identification method (Known/Introduced/ID card/ID+KBA [Exp.Date/Session ID])		
Document Type O Digital File O Paper Document	Notarization County	Document Date	Notarization Fee

Notarization Date	Signer's, Grantor's, or Maker's Name		
O Known O Introduced O ID Card/ID+KBA	Signer's, Grantor's, or Maker's mailing Address		
Exp.Date/Session ID	Brief description of the Document. If land is conveyed or charged, the name of the original grantee and the county where the land is located		
Meeting Type O Remote Online O In-Person Meeting	Introducer's, Witness's Name and Mailing address, identification method (Known/Introduced/ID card/ID+KBA [Exp.Date/Session ID])		
Document Type O Digital File O Paper Document	Notarization County	Document Date	Notarization Fee

Notarization Date	Signer's, Grantor's, or Maker's Name		
○ Known ○ Introduced ○ ID Card/ID+KBA	Signer's, Grantor's, or Maker's mailing Address Brief description of the Document. If land is conveyed or charged, the name of the original grantee and the county where the land is located		
Exp.Date/Session ID			
Meeting Type ○ Remote Online ○ In-Person Meeting	Introducer's, Witness's Name and Mailing address, identification method (Known/Introduced/ID card/ID+KBA [Exp.Date/Session ID])		
Document Type ○ Digital File ○ Paper Document	Notarization County	Document Date	Notarization Fee

Notarization Date	Signer's, Grantor's, or Maker's Name		
○ Known ○ Introduced ○ ID Card/ID+KBA	Signer's, Grantor's, or Maker's mailing Address Brief description of the Document. If land is conveyed or charged, the name of the original grantee and the county where the land is located		
Exp.Date/Session ID			
Meeting Type ○ Remote Online ○ In-Person Meeting	Introducer's, Witness's Name and Mailing address, identification method (Known/Introduced/ID card/ID+KBA [Exp.Date/Session ID])		
Document Type ○ Digital File ○ Paper Document	Notarization County	Document Date	Notarization Fee

Notarization Date	Signer's, Grantor's, or Maker's Name		
○ Known ○ Introduced ○ ID Card/ID+KBA	Signer's, Grantor's, or Maker's mailing Address Brief description of the Document. If land is conveyed or charged, the name of the original grantee and the county where the land is located		
Exp.Date/Session ID			
Meeting Type ○ Remote Online ○ In-Person Meeting	Introducer's, Witness's Name and Mailing address, identification method (Known/Introduced/ID card/ID+KBA [Exp.Date/Session ID])		
Document Type ○ Digital File ○ Paper Document	Notarization County	Document Date	Notarization Fee

Notarization Date	Signer's, Grantor's, or Maker's Name		
○ Known ○ Introduced ○ ID Card/ID+KBA	Signer's, Grantor's, or Maker's mailing Address Brief description of the Document. If land is conveyed or charged, the name of the original grantee and the county where the land is located		
Exp.Date/Session ID			
Meeting Type ○ Remote Online ○ In-Person Meeting	Introducer's, Witness's Name and Mailing address, identification method (Known/Introduced/ID card/ID+KBA [Exp.Date/Session ID])		
Document Type ○ Digital File ○ Paper Document	Notarization County	Document Date	Notarization Fee

ABOUT THE AUTHOR

TXNotaryForm.com was created by SIMARGL LLC with the aim of simplifying the process for Texas notary public applicants and notaries renewing their commission using modern technologies. As experts in the technologies needed for notary public work, we stay on top of current law changes and regulations and strive to provide the most recent and accurate information to Texas notaries. Our current book is designed for Texas notaries and covers the recent changes to the record-keeping book for Texas notaries, which will take effect on January 1st, 2025.

www.ingramcontent.com/pod product compliance
Lightning Source LLC
LaVergne TN
LVHW082359200926
848481LV00012B/3612
* 9 7 9 8 3 3 0 4 8 8 8 2 7 *